ERICKSON'S OUTDOOR ADVENTURES

DEER STANDS

ERICKSON'S OUTDOOR ADVENTURES

Series One

HUNTING

Deer Stands and Stories

Bob Erickson

Ron.
Enjoy the stories. I could
use some of yours for my
next book
Bob

ERICKSON'S OUTDOOR ADVENTURES
St. Cloud, Minnesota

ISBN: 978-1-936471-00-3

Pre-press by North Star Press of St. Cloud, Inc.

Printed in the United States of America

Published by:
Erickson's Outdoor Adventures
P.O. Box 7333
St. Cloud, Minnesota 56302
www.ericksonsoutdooradventures.com
e-mail: ericksonsoutdooradventures@gmail.com

Editor's Note

Publishing a book has been on my mind for several years, as we all have good intentions, and some succeed.

I wanted my first book to be entertaining and encouraging for youth, women, and disadvantaged people who still want to enjoy the outdoors.

This is the first of several books I plan to publish. All will promote the outdoors.

TABLE OF CONTENTS

ALL ARE SPECIAL

NO MATTER WHAT STYLE OF STAND you spend your time in, it is a special place. It could be the one your Grandpa hunted out of or the one you built out of the lumber from the old fish house. It could be as simple as the perfect branch of the big oak or as fancy as the Deer Slayer 4000 straight out of the catalog with all of the safety stickers still on it. You just know yours is the best and in the hottest spot. Right there next to the corn and bean field with the swamp, oak stand and creek close by. Your set up on the point overlooking the trails, cattails, poplars, and food plot. Fresh scrapes, beds, and rubs all over the place. This is the one with the alders, cedars, plowed field, and winter wheat right there. Should I take the big eight-point or the smaller-ten point this year? Deep down you know that you have a better chance of backing over a deer with your SUV leaving the house than you do getting a shot off at one that happens to stumble by you. But it's still your stand, in a great spot and you can't get to it fast enough.

If you do happen to get into the stand before sunrise, isn't it great to see the woods come to life. The fading of the stars, that glow of light, and all of those moving shadows. How is it that a mouse moving around makes more noise than a deer? How do they do that ghost trick? Appear and vanish at will. It always gets so cold just before sunrise. Feels great heating you up and making all of the frost sparkly. You hear those first shots ring out in the distance. Someone must have seen something, but I bet you hope they missed, because you are certain that it was "your" deer they were shooting at.

What's more annoying, the red squirrels, blue jays, or crows? Just how many swear words does a red squirrel know anyway. Although that dog barking, the electric leaf blower, and logging trucks don't help with the peace and quiet. Warm soft comfy bed at home, yet you seem to be able to sleep so much better in this rickety, cramped, falling down, freezing deer stand. Speaking of home, how is it that you cannot hear your wife ask you to take out the trash, yet out here you can clearly hear a leaf fall to the ground as well as the difference between a red and gray squirrel moving around? Your bedrooms doorknob has been broken for three years. But to have a loose board on your stand? Not going to happen! That stand gets more attention than the wife. And why do we feel the need to name our stands? Everyone in the group knows each other's stand by name and who's it is. You may not know the names of his wife or kids, but I bet you know what he calls his deer stand and the story behind it.

You can't come up with an original toast for your kid's wedding. But that shot you took! More than enough awesome, off-the-wall, top-shelf reasons why you missed. Don't use them all at once, save some for later or even next year. Speaking of the kids. Remember how excited they were to go sit with dad in the stand. You knew the chance of seeing anything was slim with all of their questions and fidgeting around, but the time together in this special place was worth it. Whoever thought that you would ever have a heater, cell phone, and blankets in your stand! The kids wanted those things. Having them out there with you was better than getting the big one. What a proud dad. They grow up so fast. Before you knew it, they want their own rifle or bow or shotgun and then their very own stand! Gun safety classes have changed quite a bit haven't they? Leaving your kid in the stand by themselves was nerve wracking, but you'd prepared them, and you knew they were ready. Tell me you had a dry eye after your son or daughter got their first deer.

You might have missed the last staff meeting at work because you didn't know which conference room it was in. But, "Meet me at ten, by the big pine where your brother's son's girl-fiend's cousin shot that big doe the year the Twins won the series. Come around that oak tree where the hawk sits and through the swamp where your dad shot those pheasants the year it snowed on the opener—that buck we saw when we were cutting shooting lanes is bedded down in there, so I should get a decent shot when you come through" is crystal clear and makes perfect sense. Speaking about work. Sitting at your desk for more than twenty minutes kills you. But staying motionless for four hours in that stand is a piece of cake. Who knew a five gallon bucket could be so comfortable. Don't you just get all third-graderish while you're sitting there? *You shoulda seen it! There was a squirrel right by my head! A doe and fawn went right under me! A chickadee landed right on my arrow! I saw two grouse, four groups of geese, a huge bear and did ya see that eagle! The frost on my gun barrel was awesome but my feet hardly got cold! I passed on two huge does! Did ya see the two shooting stars? Did you guys hear them pheasants fighting?* The wonders of nature have a way of putting it all in perspective don't they? And isn't it amazing how you always seem to see the animals and birds that you are *not* hunting at that given time. Doesn't matter that you *could* be hunting them, but the permit in your pocket is only for deer, so those fat turkeys that wander through looking barn-yard dumb, the grouse that sits above your head and looks down at you like he's invisible, and that big black bear have a free pass. If you did have permits for these guys, all you'd see is chickadees.

All those hours spent out there, don't you just come up with the most random thoughts? Everything from how old you or the kids are to that great idea you had of starting a garage floor washing service to try and retire early. Things pop into your mind and actually get thought about. How many cars have I had? When did I buy the truck. What color did the kitchen used to be. What is your first girlfriend doing now days—is she fat, does she have kids, is she a grandmother yet? What are we doing for spring break this year? How does a computer work? What are my top ten movies? How much overtime will I work this year? It is enough to make your head spin. Bringing a note pad and pen with you would be a pretty good idea. Oh, don't you just hate when any type of work, office or business stuff pops into your head! Do not even think about work or the people you work with. This is my time not works. Although, think of how much better the workplace would be if every single person there would spend some time in the outdoors. Ever go out to the stand in June or July? Looks so much different outside of deer season but still feels great. Trimming those branches that got in the way of last year's perfect shot. Speaking of the perfect shot. I can't wait until next season, because you just know that everything is going to fall into place and the chance of a lifetime will present itself. I will even be ready and better prepared this time! My deer stand is out there waiting for me and I can't get back into it fast enough.

Kevin Starr
Anoka

DAVE'S "BIG RACK" DEER SHACK

L AST YEAR IN MAY, DAVE BOMAN started his summer project. This was not an ordinary summer project. It was the Cadillac of deer stands. Dave is a farmer over from Flom, Minnesota. He loves deer hunting, but he is always thinking how he can make something bigger and better. Well, I think he finally did it for a deer stand. Sitting on twenty-plus acres of prime deer hunting ground, complete with food plot and watering holes. It was deer heaven, and Dave's heaven too!

So Dave started by getting the support beams in the ground. Then he called a concrete company to come and put concrete in the ground and also for the floor of the deer stand. The guy that came out to pour the concrete started laughing as soon as he got out of the truck because he had never poured concrete for a deer stand. Dave also dug a water hole for the deer. He plants beats, turnips, and clover for the deer to eat. Dave also had a lot of help building the shack and the site. Some people who came out actually helped, but others would sit and tell him what to do and how to do it. Some days there were more people watching than helping. It was always fun to go out to the deer stand because you never knew who would show up to help Dave or just sit around and catch up with everyone.

What started out to be an upscale deer stand morphed into a stand that has to be seen to be believed. Built entirely by friends and family it has been a group project. Dave is a farmer with fabricating skills and always seems to have a vision. He has friends and family in the roofing and steel business, electricians, and some to just lend a helping hand in whatever needs to be done. Flom is the little town "Where Friends Gather." This was certainly the case with the deer stand, which is called, "Dave's Big Rack Deer Shack."

The stand is two stories high. It has Mossy Oak steel siding, slider winders and wrought-iron deck rails. The ground floor is the garage and storage area, complete with full garage door. (You

Dave Bowman.

gotta conceal the truck when you're hunting.) The second story is the viewing/hunting area with a wrought-iron stairway and handrails. The entire viewing area has poured concrete with floor heat. A deck wraps around the front, facing the food plot and water holes. Of course there are windows on all sides for a panoramic view. A full kitchen, complete with frig and stove, and of course a sink and water. The bathroom, with a flushing potty, has a window and vanity. Oh, did I mention it has a vaulted ceiling? Or the couch

and sleeping area in the loft? Or the card table? Eventually, the inside will be tongue and groove pine, but that will be a winter project . . . Dave's gotta get some farming' done too!

Once it started to get dark, we would start a bonfire and stand around and have some beverages. Everyone would talk about how once Dave got the deer stand done, it would be so cool. They could go hunting and not have to freeze their butts off.

The deer stand was finished before the 2009 hunting season. Dave let his Uncle Raymond Buschette, Mic Buschette, and many others sit in the stand. Dave's Uncle Raymond got the first deer out of the stand the first weekend of deer hunting. During the week, Dave let anyone who wanted come to his stand. So some of Dave's family and friends went to the deer stand, trying to get the "big" buck. Then, on the weekend Dave finally got out of the field so he took some kids who had never been hunting up to the stand just to show them what hunting was all about.

This past April 10th, it was so nice out a group of us went four-wheeling. While we were four-wheeling, we got a call from Dave. He was working in the field and was going to be done very soon. He wanted us all to go to the deer shack. So, we all said, yes, we would do that. We got to the shack, and Dave was still on the combine. There were some people with us who had never been on a combine. Dave told them to get in, and he would take them around in the machine. Then the rest of us went to the shack, and there was Bev Wang, and she had brought us out some food. We had some hot dogs and made a bonfire in front of the shack.

Dave would like to give a big thank you to Bev Wang, John and Renne Nysetvold, James and Kaia Askelson, Mic and Blanch Buschette, Kelvin and Margie Kruger, Matt Boman, Peni Rasmusson, Seth and RaChelle Boman, T.J. Stevens, Taylor Wang, Scott and Jill Boman, Darin Williams, Jeff Lunde, and John Petrick. I know I'm missing some people, and I'm sorry, but you know that Dave appreciates your help. This made our effort all worthwhile.

Dave Boman Flom
Deb Buschette
Detroit Lakes

MY FIRST STAND

It was 1976 and it was my first deer hunt. My Uncle Kleo had 300 acres of great hunting land near McGregor. Kleo, Russ (my older brother), and I had spent many hours in the woods to prepare for the upcoming hunt. This would be Russ's third unsuccessful hunting season if he did not harvest one this year. I felt my first season would not be fruitful because, if my older brother had not gotten one, then I surely wouldn't. How wrong I was!

I still did not know which gun I would be using as I did not own one. I was a little worried about the kick. I knew some guns kicked more than others, and, at thirteen, I was afraid of that.

After a supper of chili and chocolate cake, we went with my uncle to his cabin. Kleo lived in the Cities and would come up every weekend. His place was only three miles away, so preparations for the next day's hunt were only minutes away. After we put our gear away and made sure our boots would be warm and dry for the morning, we gathered around the table as if this were the moment we were waiting for. Kleo would give us a chance to choose coffee or cranberry/apple juice to drink. I always picked the cranberry/apple juice. I never knew why, but my brother sometimes took coffee, but I don't think he liked it. At first the conversation was just some small talk, and then it went to guns. I knew there was a 303 army rifle, a 30/30, and a 32 Winchester that were available to use. Russ bought his own 30/30, and Kleo used a 30/06 with a scope. I was afraid I would get the army rifle. It looked mean and was sure to give a wallop with its metal butt plate. The bullets were huge!

Kleo walked over to where the guns were and came back with the 32 Winchester. He started to show me the gun and how the safety mechanisms worked. I fell in love with it right away. It was short and exactly the right size for a youth to hunt with. Not too heavy, but kind of hard to load. Kleo handed me one bullet when I asked how many it could hold in the magazine. He then told me I would get only "one" bullet, and he waited about ten seconds to see what my reaction would be. I knew my brother's magazine would hold six shells, but none of this was bothering me as I felt I was holding a piece of gold in that one bullet.

As Kleo reached into his pocket, I heard a noise that made me look up. I could see my brother and uncle smiling as Kleo held out his hand with more of the gold. He said, "Here are six more, just in case." It was then that he told me what my grandpa had always said, "It takes only one bullet, if you are patient and wait for a good clean kill."

There was more small talk about the hunt to come and then it was off to bed. Sleep? Yeah right. Like I could sleep after all this! I felt as if I had made some passage of rights or was inducted into some fraternity of hunters all over the world. I was about to go on my first hunt! I did succumb to sleep sometime later and was awakened by the sweet smell of coffee, bacon, eggs, and the smell of wood smoke. Those smells would forever remind me of some of the best times I have ever had.

We quickly jumped out of bed and went downstairs where Kleo had breakfast waiting. There was some more small talk and what to do if we would get a deer, and then it was time to go. We each had about half a mile walk that I will never forget. Gun in hand, loaded, on safe, we headed out to our spots. I was afraid of the dark, but the gun gave me some reassurance. The morning was cold as I made it to my ground blind. Russ always hunted from the same stand, which was about half a mile walk through the hay fields and woods. Kleo would walk down by the river, and I would be in the southeast corner of his large field. My stand was actually a ground blind and consisted of a cleared area at the base of a small oak. A two-by-four-by two-foot board was nailed onto the oak as a rest for my gun. From my ground blind, I could sit or stand up and see out over the plowed hayfields or look down a mowed trail that went about fifty yards before it meandered into the woods. I had cleared some brush a few weeks earlier for a shooting lane also. The shooting lane ended at a swamp. Behind it were some good trails.

My uncle told me to watch the trail to the north, and every once in a while look back at the field. He also said how, at this time of the year, bucks were chasing does. If a doe were to come out, that was a good thing, especially if she had no fawns with her. This meant she had chased them away and was be ready for a buck. "When you see a doe, you want to watch where she was as there may be a buck following her. Even up to half an hour later," he told us.

Only about twenty minutes after shooting had started, I stared at the field for about four minutes. When I turned back, there was a large doe. The doe I saw was the largest I have ever seen even to this day. At first I was sure it was a horse. She slowly walked into the woods and headed toward my brother's stand. His stand was

Ground blind with truck air-ride seat.

about a quarter mile away. I had been sitting, but now I was crouching on my knees in anticipation of the buck that was sure to follow. One thing I had learned at a young age—my uncle was smart. If he said a buck would follow, I believed him. Time went by, and after fifteen minutes, my heart finally slowed down to a natural rhythm. Fifteen more minutes found me questioning my uncle's words. This doe was by herself, or had her fawns moved through the trail while I was watching the field? Either way, my eyes were glued to the spot, and it was then that I realized how tense I was. Forty-five minutes passed, and my knees and feet were falling asleep from kneeling on them, so I stood up. I shut my eyes for only a second. And it was as if a ghost of a buck had appeared where the doe had been standing only forty-six minutes earlier. He was broad and wide like a Guernsey bull. The rack was impressive, and it was thick and big around like his shoulders. I slowly raised my gun up only when his nose was to the ground. At any moment I expected him to look right at me as my heart was beating so loud.

I set the lever action hammer back into fire, and it made its familiar *click*. The open sites found the buck and I squeezed the trigger. The roar of the blast made me blink, and when I opened my eyes there was a lot of smoke from the barrel, but no buck! I sprinted to where he had been and when I had crossed the first thirty of the fifty yards, I could see his antlers sticking up out of the two-foot-high grass. He was trying to get up! I walked cautiously up to him and shot again, and again. When I went around to his back side I nudged him with the barrel. Then I noticed how truly magnificently big he was. I hooted, hollered, and yelled so loud that my brother heard me over at his stand. I was very lucky to have gotten him as I hit him in his ear and broke his antler with my first shot. This dazed him and put him on the ground. Out of all the other shots I took from 10 yards or less, only one bullet found its mark, as we later found out. Buck fever must have set in at the moment. I had no idea what to do next, so I walked the half mile up to the cabin. My uncle was already in. He said after the shots he came in right away. He asked me if I got one, and I said, "Yes, and a big one too." We started up the Ford 4000, hooked up the wagon and drove out there to get him. My uncle was impressed with the size and got to work gutting him. When we tried to lift him into the trailer it was a real struggle as he weighed 220 pounds. He was a non-typical ten-pointer with one drop tine.

When my brother came up from his stand, he had this love/hate/envious look on his face. He was happy for me but mad at me also. This same look was to happen many more times as I have been lucky enough to shoot many other large bucks over these past thirty-three years. He finally did harvest his first buck after six seasons, and it was a spike.

Pictures taken with an old camera and were very blurry to say the least. My uncle was taking the venison to the Cities to get it processed. At the last second, my brother said he wanted the antlers for rattling as he had read about this in a magazine. No one told me to keep the rack for anything, so I told him sure. He sawed them off at the base and later lost one. There was one left that I used in shop class to create a knife handle in seventh grade. The old photos and the knife, along with some great memories are what I have left. The knife handle was his brow tine and was eight inches long and had a four-and-one-quarter-inch circumference at the base. It dwarfed anything I have shot since. Three impressive shoulder mounts are on my walls, and none has the base, size, or length of my first buck from my first "stand." The following year I upgraded by buying a 243 Ithaca and adding a welded stand that had room for a board as a chair. This was attached to my oak. The two-by-four was taken down, and the bark cleared away so I could carve my initials in the tree.

Not only was this my first stand, it was my first hunt, and my first deer. I have shot many deer since that time, but I have never gotten one as big. I will always remember my first stand. It taught me that big bucks (dollars) need not be spent on your stand to get the big buck. Kleo gave that gun to me many years later. I still love it, and I hope to use it again some day. Who knows, maybe I will get another trophy when I do.

Brad Hageman

Foley, Minnesota

FORTRESS STAND

My good neighbor has this grain bin and I had this brainstorm to make a deer stand out if it. I took the top off it first. We ran rods (rebar) through it about three feet down from the top and horizontally across for support for the floor. Then we put a heavy wire mesh grill on top of the rebar rods.

When we aren't using the stand, we leave the bottom panel open, so water can drain.

The biggest job was loading and unloading the grain bin on our sixteen-foot car-hauler trailer to get it out to the field where we wanted to put it. It took three of us for this to set it up and approximately two hours. We put a heavy chain around the bin and pulled it up and off the trailer slowly with the tractor and loader bucket. We put it on a hill about three hundred feet from a ten-acre willow swamp where we would always see a Big Buck. There weren't any trees around to build a stand, so we had to have some kind of free-standing one.

We also drove stakes around the legs and fastened them to each other for security and added a different ladder.

It did pay off for me. I got an eight-point buck that weighted about 175 pounds. I hope to get a bigger one next year.

Elroy Knauer
Cologne, Minnesota

LEARNING EXPERIENCE

I was excited for my first deer hunt to start. We were hunting on our farm and were up at 6:00 the first morning, and after a quick breakfast, we headed out to our stands.

I was hunting with Grandpa, and he instructed me that, if I had something to say, to poke him and then whisper.

Getting to our stand before sunrise, we climbed up and waited. Grandpa told me to watch for deer, but I had to limit my movements. If I saw a deer, I again had to poke him.

We had no action, and soon Grandpa was giving off zzz's. I thought this might scare the deer, but I didn't dare wake him. When he woke up, I didn't tell him he had been snoring.

By noon we had seen or heard nothing, and we walked back to the farm for dinner. After a quick meal, we headed back to our stand. Waiting until the end of shooting time, we still saw nothing. I thought deer hunting would be exciting. This wasn't.

We went out again the next morning, but I decided to split from Grandpa. I was only eleven years old, but Grandpa had taught me safety and to respect my common sense. Telling me to hunt safely, Grandpa wished me good luck.

Knowing the terrain, I walked a short distance to a ditch and sat on a log. I had been there only a short time when, out of nowhere, a doe came dashing over a hill on the other side of the ditch.

I stood up, raised the gun, aimed at the heart and pulled the trigger. Nothing happened. I had forgotten to take off the safety. Grandpa had taught me gun safety well, but not shooting.

As I watched my first deer bound over the hill, my heart was beating like drum. Sitting back on the log, I relived my mistake.

Going back to Grandpa, I told him about the deer that got away. He felt sorry for me but said that my experience was part of hunting education.

Getting back to the farm, everyone could tell by the look on my face that something had happened. Everyone wanted the story. I told it, knowing I would never make that particular mistake again.

Boone Matzke
Rochester, Minnesota

By Dodge

Enclosed is a photo of the buck deer I got on the last day of the season back in 2007, the year we built our deer stand. I got this deer with a 30/30 Dodge Caravan at 4:00 a.m. on Highway 65 just south of the town of Mora, Minnesota. I was on my way to pick up Pete for our final day of the rifle season going forty miles per hour when, all of a sudden, this deer came bolting across the highway. I saw the deer, slammed on my brakes and thought I was going to miss it, well almost. I just clipped it in the hind leg on the right side and broke its leg.

Down into the ditch went the deer. I stopped right away, marked the spot where the deer was hit, put on my four-way lights on the shoulder, got out my lantern and went to look for the deer. It's quite dark at 4:00 a.m. I couldn't find the deer. I thought it would be lying in the ditch, dead, but no deer. I then drove to Pete's house, told him what happened. Pete said, "I'll fix breakfast and wait until daylight, then you can go look for the deer."

After breakfast, it was getting light, so drove over to where I marked the spot on the highway and starting looking for this deer. I spotted it lying down right off of the ditch, a few feet into the woods, still alive, but wounded. Well, I thought, I've got a legal deer license, and I've got my rifle with me, but I thought seeing I was within fifty yards of town, I'd better get hold of the sheriff. I drove to the sheriff's office, talked to the dispatcher and she said that she'd call a deputy and give him the location to meet me. I then drove back to that location. Within ten minutes the deputy arrived. I pointed out the deer to the deputy, and he could see that it was wounded. He drew his weapon and shot the deer in the neck to put him down. After dressing out the deer, the deputy helped me drag it to the shoulder of the road. The deputy gave me a road-kill permit. I told many friends that I got my deer with a 30/30 Dodge Caravan. It was clear to them I hit this deer with very little damage to my Caravan. I then called my hunting partner, Pete, and he brought his pickup truck over to the scene. We loaded the deer into his truck, drove it over to my place and hung it up to cool.

We then proceeded to our deer hunting stand for the day. The next day, Monday, I skinned out the deer, boned it out, made several portions from the deer, and we shared the meat. All the meat was delicious. We didn't get any deer at our deer stand that year, but we had meat in the freezer, the hard way.

Vince Shallbetter
Mora, Minnesota

Vince.

CHANGES

AT AGE THIRTEEN I MEASURED MY hunting success by the size of the antlers and how many deer were bagged. One time I literally had to measure an antler to see if I had a buck (three-inch tines) or I would have to use my doe permit. I was only a thirteen-year-old, but I was already hooked on hunting.

For me it was an older brother and an uncle who got me into hunting. Many stories and hours afield led to an appreciation for the outdoors and the majestic animals that called the woods their home. My favorite time afield was just observing the habits of the elusive whitetail. I would physically check where the deer would go after I lost sight of them so I could later know the escape routes for future hunts. I found it interesting how they would snort when I was detected. I would try to mimic this sound in hopes that I could confuse them. Needless to say, this did not work. I also came to realize that deer were habitual and liked trails and bedding areas year after year. It took me about fifteen years to realize that success did not come in numbers of deer shot but in how the hunt took place and who was part of the hunt. There came a day that our hunting party grew and included people who I did not know. This seemed like an intrusion into a sacred tradition and I was not happy.

On one of the hunts, it was a very warm, windy day, which blew my scent into the woods where the deer drivers would be within the hour. This drive was bigger than any we had ever had before. There were seven hunters instead of our traditional three. I was at the base of a huge pine on the edge of a spruce bog where there was sure to be a trophy buck. So I was hoping. I was very excited at the prospects of the drive that would begin in an hour. It was at this time that an odd-antlered buck headed into the wind and lay down about one hundred feet away from me in the tall grass. I was hiding more than usual as now there was a deer bedded just yards away.

An hour later, the drive was on, and many does ran out across the eighty-acre field to my left. It was now my turn as the drive should be pushing through my woods. I took a peek around the big pine just in time to see a large deer's rear end go back into the woods away from me.

"Had it scented me? Was it the buck I saw an hour ago?" I came to the conclusion (hoped) that it was a large buck and would be pushed back to me in the drive. Here came a doe, running so close that I could have clubbed her with the

gun. By now my heart was in my throat, and it felt as if there were a bass drum in my chest. Then out came the driver who was new to hunting and the party. I motioned to him that he should go over to where I saw the one-antlered buck lie down. He seemed confused as to what I wanted, so I prompted him a little more with more hand gestures which my uncle and brother would have recognized from a hundred yards away. He took about twenty more steps, and up jumped the buck. I was quick to get my scope on it as it ran towards the large ditch near my pine. I squeezed the trigger, and down he went. As I walked over to the buck, it was then that I noticed the other tine was bent down along the jaw line. The new hunter walked over and said, "You sure nailed that one." The usual excitement was there, but then disappointment followed when I was sharing it with someone I did not know. It was awkward to say the least. This was the last time we hunted with my uncle and his growing extended family of hunters. It was very different and difficult the following year not to do the same routines that were part of our prior hunting experiences. At this time I realized success was not just harvesting a buck or doe, but who was with you to share in it.

By now I had three young kids of my own, and most of my time afield was spent with them, so it was time anyhow to start my own traditions. I now measure success in how I can help my kids learn to respect the woods and to love hunting. Muzzle loading has given me the chance to hunt again for myself, as I have six kids who will be keeping me busy for at least ten more years.

Brad Hageman
Foley, Minnesota

GRANDPA'S MEMORIES

THE IDEA BEHIND THE STAND CAME together because we wanted to put my grandpa's last pickup cab in his favorite deer-hunting spot on the farm. The problem was that we wanted to leave all the glass in the cab and still be able to shoot out of it in all directions. After many ideas, we came up with the one to make the cab rotate on the tripod. It worked out great, and it didn't make any noise and stops at any point we want. I've spent many hours hunting out of the stand with family and friends hunting deer and coyotes. My cousin shot the first buck out of the Roadhunter last year on the family farm.

We built four stands altogether. They are all spread out across the family farm here in Ashby, Minnesota. Two of the stands are on tripods, and the other two have wheels so we can move them around.

Sam Balgaard
Ashby, Minnesota

Inside cab.

FIRST DEER

M Y FIRST EXPERIENCE DEER HUNTING was when I was ten years old and with my Uncle Mike. We were hunting the river bottoms near Henderson, Minnesota. Mike had just built the stand that summer. It was big enough for two people to sit in, and it was about twenty feet up in a tall tree.

On opening day of deer hunting, my dad, Nathan, woke me up to shower and get my hunting clothes on. Mike picked me up at four o'clock in the morning to go hunting.

When we got to the river bottoms, we had to walk about

300 yards to get to the deer stand. We climbed up into the stand around five o'clock. We had seen two deer that morning, but they were too far away to shoot. We tried calling them closer, but had no luck.

After sitting patiently and calling all afternoon, I gave my .410 shotgun to Mike to hold because I was getting tired and lay down on the floor of the stand to rest.

About twenty minutes later, Mike heard a rustle in the leaves and turned quietly to see what it was. He was surprised to see a deer coming.

Mike gave me a nudge, and I got up quietly and was surprised and excited to see the deer walking right towards us.

I didn't take my gun from Mike because I was worried the deer would run off in the other direction, so I started aiming the gun while Mike was holding it. The deer came within ten feet. I pulled the trigger. The deer jumped and ran about fifty yards and dropped under another hunter's stand.

It was unbelievable, exciting, and the first deer hunting experience of my life. It was a 122-pound doe.

Andrew Lind
Jordan, Minnesota

REALLY CLOSE! 1959

S OMEONE ASKED ME ONE TIME, "How close have you come to a deer while you're hunting it?" Here was my answer:

Many years ago, in 1959, I used to hunt with a group of fellas in the Grand Rapids, Minnesota, area. Actually we were north of Grand Rapids on Highway 38 to the Suomi Country. We would rent a cabin from a old Finlander by Graves Lake. Emil Hokenan was the owner, and he'd fire up his Finnish sauna for us to use and enjoy on opening evening after our hunt. What a treat. Wow!

During those days, it was common to make deer drives. There were eight hunters and we'd put four guys on stands, and then the other four guys would make a drive from one to two miles long from the standers.

I'd hunted is those woods and was taught well from the master, Link Obert, a friend of my dad's who was born and raised in Deer River, Minnesota, area and was a guide for many lodges back in the 1930s. There weren't any roads into that area in those years, so the deer hunters had to take a train to those hunting lodges. Link Obert was one of the guides, and he knew the woods very well. My dad wasn't a deer hunter and told Link that shooting a deer was like shooting a cow in a pasture. Dad was a meat man and owned his own meat market.

Link would tell my dad, "Bob, if you see just how fast those deer run, you'd know you've never see a cow run that fast." Well, this one day of deer hunting, we were going to make a deer drive. Link would take three fellas with him, and he would place them at a deer stand. I would take three fellas with me for the drivers. I'd line them up on a gravel road in a straight line and give them directions. On this one drive, we were headed south. Everyone had a compass and knew how to use it. I'd be the last one to line up and would holler to the hunter next to me, "Okay" and that hunter would holler, "Okay" to the next hunter, and on down the line.

27

Before I lined up, I told them if they got confused on the drive as to the direction, they should just remember to go south, not north or west, but for sure, "DON'T GO EAST." I knew the lay of the land and east of this driving area was a old railroad bed that had been abandoned many years ago. The locomotive and coal car had been going down this railway, came to a curve in the track, and was going way too fast. They had jumped the tracks and ended up in the swamp. The conductor and coal man had crawled out of this train, walked the tracks back to town, Marcel, Minnesota. The next day, a team of men got another locomotive, with a flat car and a crain on the flat car to pull the train out of the swamp. When they got to the area where the train had jumped the tracks, there wasn't any locomotive or coal car. It had sunk out of sight. They put the train in reverse, went back to town and never used that line again. I knew where that sink hole was and didn't want anyone to end up there, that's why I was so firm on giving directions about not going east on this drive.

I proceeded to make my drive south, went about fifteen to twenty minutes, and then had a call of mother nature. So, at the bottom of a little dry swamp, I stopped to do my duty. I heard what I thought was a deer walking or a man walking to my west. All of a sudden there was a deer hunter walking right towards me headed east. Lo and behold that hunter was one of ours, one of the drivers. I couldn't believe it. He didn't see me until I hollered at him. I said to him, "Where are you going?"

"Oh," he said. "I got confused and turned around in the woods and couldn't remember which way I was supposed to go. I remember you said something about east, so that's the way I was headed."

I told him, "*Don't* go east. I'll wait here for ten minutes. You go west for ten minutes, stop and then head south. I'll wait right here for ten minutes and then start south, so we'll both be on track to complete this deer drive together."

Within five minutes, over the hill from the southeast, a buck deer came running at full bore headed right toward me. I put my open sights of my 30/30 right on him and said to myself, "Keep running my way and I hold off from firing any shots at you, but if you turn away from me, I'll open up and fire."

All of a sudden the deer was getting closer to me, and I thought I'd better start shooting or I'll get run over. The first shot hit him in the back, just off his spine. I saw the hole open up on his back. That didn't stop him. He kept coming towards me. I took a side-step back, dropped my rifle to my side, and he ran right next to me. I fired the second shot when he ran past me, and I saw another hole open up on his side. Blood squirted all over my pants. He continued to run away from me with his back to me. I aimed at the back of his head, pulled the trigger and, *whambo*, he dropped like a ton of bricks. *Wow*, I thought, *that was really some exciting action.*

I dressed him out, then dragged him north to my vehicle, loaded him up and drove back to the standers, so they wouldn't be looking for me on the drive. Now that's about as close as it gets. I figured that driver I sent on the right direction probably kicked that deer out of his bed, and he headed in my direction. One never knows what action can happen on a deer drive.

Vince Shallbetter
Mora, Minnesota

HER FIRST HUNT

MEG'S FIRST HUNT WAS WHEN SHE was sixteen years old. I had to work Saturday morning so we were late getting to the hunting land. One of my sons (ten years old) was pouting because he could not come out with me. He was staring out the large picture window at a very windy late afternoon. We were busy getting on our clothes to make the last hour of hunting when my pouty boy said, "There's a deer out there." Still in a pouty voice he announces, "It's a big one, and I think it's a buck."

I ran to the window and there was a very nice buck standing a quarter mile away. My mind started to race, and I began scheming how we could go to the north and wait for him to come to us, when my daughter said, "Can't we just shoot him from here?"

"Well, no. That isn't hunting," I told her. As we made our way outside, we crouched over to the hay bales that were our van-

Jon and Meg.

tage point. The buck ran to the north but then stopped 250 yards away and stood in the clearing for an eternity. It was as if the buck was meant for her. About this time I decided that there was no way we were going to get in front of him as he was on the very edge of our field. I also made the decision to shoot from the hay bales as her gun (a 243 Ithaca) was dead on at 200 yards. I was using my brother's 30-30 and knew I would be shooting (lobbing) the bullets sixteen feet high, so it was all up to her. As we were looking through our scopes, I was telling her where to aim and to hold the butt of the gun snuggly into her shoulder. All the while the buck just stood there broadside to us. I actually told her to aim at the middle of the shoulder and then said to aim two inches lower than the back of the buck. I told her to slowly squeeze the trigger and continue to breathe.

When the gun belched forth its deadly assailant, I was busy watching the buck through the 30-30 scope with no intentions of shooting. I asked her if she was going to shoot again as the buck whirled towards us in a large loop back to where we first saw it. It was then that I looked up at her, and she was watching it with her eyes with this big smile on her face. I shouted to shoot again, but I could tell she was not going to, so I grabbed the gun and let one fly at the running buck.

Meg's training was good and we were to find out shortly how good it was. Usually I would wait half an hour or longer before approaching a deer, but the sun was going down so we walked to where she shot the buck. There was a little snow dusting the ground, but we could easily see where the buck started to run. Upon closer inspection we found the running tracks and a little blood. The buck had run into a small island of woods, and we did not see it come out the other side. I told Meg to go around the back side and I would walk through the 100 feet of woods and brush in hopes of pushing it out to her if it was still in there. I was following the blood trail and just entered the woods, when I saw him. There he was fully dispatched. Upon checking closer I hollered for her to come on over. I pretended that the buck had run the other direction so I told her to track it as I had. She followed the trail and came to the buck and got very excited. When we butchered the deer, we only found one bullet hole, and it was on the side that Meg shot at so my desperation shot had been futile and she had the killing one. Her first outing was almost as lucky as my first one, but my deer had been a much bigger one and non typical. This buck was a very nice eight-pointer with really long legs.

She ended up with the biggest buck for the season and was entitled to the master bed at the hunting cabin the following season. Sorry to say, she has not hunted since as school and life got in the way. Now, eleven years later, and she is married and will probably get her husband into the sport of hunting also.

Brad Hageman
Foley, Minnesota

REAL COMFORT

IT WAS ONE OF THOSE THINGS THAT my dad had mentioned around the daily (during deer season, and some pre-season) weenie/hot-dog roast for a couple of years. How having a fully enclosed stand would sure be a nice place to be more comfortable during deer season and poor weather. Despite his other stand for the past twenty years, one that had a wood stove for warmth, was fully enclosed with a full 360-degree view would sure be nice. Something like an eight-by-twelve-foot building with a shingled roof.

Then, in the fall of 2003, things just came together and lined up right one day. My dad (a carpenter by trade) had collected a few windows and materials from different spots and bought a large load of returned treated lumber for a very low price. He had the large round-top Marvin window (picked up for fifty dollars since the outer pane of the round-top was cracked), the large window on the other side, and a glass door all sitting around, the large load of treated lumber he had picked up, a good load of lumber from a deck we tore down, and left-over shingles.

He called me up in early October and said he was going to build a deer stand and put it down the ridge a ways from where he had been sitting the past few years (and where the weenie/hot-dog fire had been). And he had decided to do it right (like he'd talked about). Over the next two weekends he built (mostly by himself) the stand from the ground up. It was brought to the point of having no windows, shingles, or transport method while sitting in the yard.

During that last frantic weekend (the one before deer opener) of building, we (him, his cousin, and myself) finished it off. We shingled the roof, tied the posts and bracing all together to two large white-oak skids that we had sawed for pulling it to its destination, built the six-by-fourteen deck and stairs separate from the stand, built two other six-by-six elevated box stands, pulled the stand to its location, located and leveled it, installed all the windows once it was in location, attached the deck and stairs, and installed the wood stove and its chimney pipe.

At this point it was ready to hunt in for the fall of 2003. However, it had plywood sheeting on the outside and simple framed walls on the inside. The solid maple interior, and cedar shake siding would follow in the next two years.

In 2004, I bought a house in Breckenridge, Minnesota, that had a large stack of maple flooring in the garage, some bundled, some loose, and some had been wet in the flood of 1997, all shorter lengths (up to four feet at the very longest).

Aaron and Ed.

I didn't know what to do with it all, so we came up with the idea of using it for the interior of the deer stand and building a table out of the bird's-eye pieces for the deer stand as well. All of the maple was hand-planed on site and installed and varnished over the course of two very long weekends. It got to be a very long job with all the small pieces and going around the windows by the time it was done it took almost as long as the original construction of the stand did. However, after it was finished, it looked great and was a great use of the wood. (The maple did enclose a few beer cans and other treasures within the walls from the first year. Maybe we'll un-tomb them someday, maybe not.)

Also in 2004 my dad installed the storage/bed compartments in the one end of the stand. It is a large bench with full storage under the lid for miscellaneous items and the bedding. The flaps on the outside of the bench came up and were supported by the ladder-like item that hung on the wall over the bench. The bed is forty inches by eight feet when folded out. It's all finished with birch.

In 2005, I was tired of looking at the plywood sheeting and decided that hand-split cedar shingles would make very nice siding. So, mixed into three weekends that fall, I completed the siding with the help of my dad and one of my cousins. It really helped complete the right look. It's constructed of almost all wood products with a wood stove that makes it just right for relaxing and hunting in the woods of Minnesota.

Somewhere in all of this we installed an inverter for a twelve-volt battery to run the fluorescent lights. We get up to sixteen hours of running the lights, radio, whatever we needed out of one trolling-motor battery charge. Also installed is a removable three-burner propane stove from a camper for easier cooking than on the wood stove when some of the younger kids come for breakfast before light, or when we want something other than roasted weenies (the weenie fire is now permanently next to this stand) and is lit after dark.

All told there is very little cash invested in the stand, just a lot of time. Of course MANY other ideas were thrown out during the construction and since it was completed—drive in underneath, enclosed for bunks and more central heating underneath, automated everything. One of the best things is that my dad still sees/gets big deer from it as the attached picture shows!

Jason Moses
Breckenridge, Minnesota

Keegan Moses.

HOUSE ON THE PRAIRIE

F ALL HAD COME EARLY THIS YEAR bringing with it a chill, and today was no different. Friday the thirtieth dawned cloudy, cold and rainy. After working most of the morning, I soon made plans to head out to my tree stand.

I went home to shower and dress, then I grabbed the hunting bow and headed for my uncle's woods. I arrived and decided to hunt in the new double-ladder stand that my uncle and had put up earlier in the season. By five o'clock the wind began to strengthen. Rain and twenty- to twenty-five-mile-an-hour winds forced me to rethink my strategy. I left the stand and headed west about ten miles to my dad's neck of the woods to finish the hunt. With the rain falling steadily on my pickup, I decided that I would rather stay dry and sit in the hunting shack and wait it out for any action. Pulling in the driveway I saw Dad putting burgers on the grill. With only a good half-hour left of daylight, I left quickly, telling him that I was headed for the hunting shack.

The hunting shack had been planned after my dad and step-mom purchased a seventy-acre farm with great wooded property. Ideas had immediately popped into our heads to install a rustic shack, complete with a picturesque pond at the top of the woods, the place of any hunting dreams. My dad, brother, and I were excited to begin this project. While working later on an old barn roof, we had all realized that Dad's rustic shack could be built of the wood and beams from the barn. The hunting shack would then be cost efficient plus have the barn wood beauty and character.

We had no problem finding the motivation to tear down the rest of the barn and to build the sixteen-by-twenty-foot hunting shack. Windows reclaimed from a trailer home and installed in the shack helped make the pond visible. A loft for sleeping, wood stove for heat and making coffee and plenty of deer stories made the shack complete. It was now ready for hunters looking for a place to stay dry.

With the thought of staying warm and limited daylight I had left that day, I hurried up to the shack. Heading up the porch I paused. Looking over the pond, I spied a deer far off in the bean field. At 150 yards, she began to move. I watched and quietly slipped in the front door. I opened a window and got situated to wait, but the doe wandered off.

Fifteen minutes later, a nice eight-point buck appeared opposite the window I had opened. I tried the bleat call to persuade the buck to come closer. Through the back door, I watched as he stood motionless. I decided to pass on this small buck. At this time I checked the clock, 6:15 p.m. That only left me seventeen minutes of legal shooting light that day. I positioned myself back by the front door, overlooking the porch and pond. Suddenly I noticed another good-sized deer about eighty yards from the shack. As I reached for the binoculars, I realized that this deer was a nice, big eight-point! I grabbed my grunt call, quickly gave two grunts, but received no reaction. Between the steady rain, the wind, and the whispering of the tall grasses, he couldn't hear the calls. I grunted one last time as loudly as I could. Suddenly his direction changed. He began heading slowly towards the shack.

I grabbed my bow and watched him until he was fifty yards out. I then drew my bow and had it positioned out the window that I had opened earlier. The buck continued on and began crossing the pond dike. Once the buck came into view of my sites I blew a soft bleat. He stopped. Now at full draw, I let the arrow fly. I watched the buck scamper away. I knew I had made contact but wasn't sure where!

Ten minutes later, I walked out to check the spot twenty-five yards away from the shack where I hit the buck. As I walked out in the wind and rain, I found no sign of blood, tracks, or my arrow. Nerves started to kick in as I walked to my dad's to share the news and organize the family to help search for the deer.

As I walked into the house, the stunned look on my face must have showed I had something to share. I greeted my dad and

brother with the news that I just shot a buck through the window of the shack. After calling my wife and brother-in-law we finally had enough of a crew to search for the deer.

By now two hours had passed, so we walked in the direction where I had last seen the deer. My step-mom volunteered to take the four-wheeler in the opposite direction and to check out the distant hayfield. But as she walked up the trail towards the four-wheeler, she came across the buck about fifty yards from the hunting shack. There he was! Nestled in the wet grass, he lay motionless. He was a nice eight-point buck, about 220 pounds, and his rack displayed a wide spread—twenty-one and one-half inches—with fourteen-inch tines. This eight-pointer was magnificent!

I couldn't believe it!

It felt like the hunting shack had come full circle. All the plans, work, and time spent in it helped create a hunting story created from its very own walls and windows.

Lincoln Mehrkens
Goodhue, Minnesota

DOUBLE DEER
DOUBLE TROUBLE

S OMEONE ASKED ME: HOW MANY DEER have you shot at one time? That brings back an old memory. While deer hunting in 1960 in the Suomi Country, north of Grand Rapids, Minnesota on Highway 38, I went to my deer stand on opening day. Not seeing any deer that morning, I thought I'd take a hike down a old logging road to see if I could spot any. At one point in the road, I stopped and looked to my right where there was a large hill going straight up to the east. I looked up that hill and wondered what the top of that hill looks like. Up the hill I went, and when I got to the top I found beautiful country with very little underbrush and many mature trees. I then built a ground deer stand with a few windfall trees up against one of those mature trees. I cleared an area around my stand of leaves and sat down, rifle across my lap. Shortly thereafter I dozed off. I roused when I heard something running in the leaves. I thought it sounded like a couple of squirrels headed my way. Was I surprised when two deer appeared—a large doe and her fawn. We had no snow that year for opening. I picked up my rifle, took aim at the doe and fired. Nothing happened. I shot again and again and finally hit her in the lungs. She hunched up and started tip toeing down the hill that she just came up with a very pronounced blood trail behind her. Meanwhile, the fawn just stayed by her mother, jumping straight up and down as if she was saying, "Mommy's hurt. What should I do?" I helped her out with that decision. My next shot put the fawn down. I was then out of bullets, but knew that I had one more shell in my kidney pack, which I wore on my back side on a belt. I took off the belt and kidney pack, dumped the contents on the ground among the leaves looking for that last bullet to go after my doe to finish her off. At last, I found that bullet, put it into the chamber and proceeded to follow the blood trail of the doe that I had originally shot. I had just started over the hill when I heard a shot ring out at the bottom of the hill, and I thought, *Oh no, someone shot my doe*. I ran down the hill as fast as I could, following that blood trail right up to my doe lying dead on the ground. There was a deer hunter cradling his gun standing close by. As I came up to my doe, I said to the stranger, "Thanks for finishing off my deer," and he said, "What do you mean *your* deer? I shot it last!" I then told him that the old rule of the woods was that, when someone shoots a deer and it's a fatal shot, the person who drew first blood claims ownership. That's what took place here. I said to him, "Look at that blood trail coming down the hill. That's from my original shot."

"Well, I don't know about that," the hunter said, still cradling his rifle. "I shot this deer, and I got the final kill so, to me, it's my deer."

Just then, the doe made a twitching move, and I used my last shell to shoot her in the head. "There," I said. "I just got the final shot as well as the first shot. Therefore it's my deer according to your rules." I then took off my coat, rolled up my shirt sleeves, took out my knife and proceeded to dress out the deer. This hunter continued just to stand there cradling his gun, saying no more. All of a sudden four of this guy's buddies appeared and asked, "What's going on here?"

I explained the situation to one of the older hunters, and after a bit of discussion, it was decided and agreed that a flip of the coin would decide just who would end up with this deer. Luck was on my side. I called heads on the coin flip, and it came up heads. I then put a rope around the deer's head and started to drag it out to the highway, where I had my vehicle parked. As I was dragging the deer, I overheard the guy who had flipped the coin say, "Darn it, that's the second deer I lost this weekend due to a flip of a coin."

After dragging my doe to the truck and loading it up, I then went back up the hill, dressed out the fawn and dragged that deer to the truck. I brought both deer to our deer camp. I tagged my doe, and one of the other fellas put his tag on the fawn.

This was considered party hunting for this other hunting pal was just down the hill from where all the action took place. During those early days, there wasn't such a thing as doe permits. You went deer hunting to shoot a deer, either a buck or a doe. Those were the days!

Vincent Shallbetter
Mora, Minnesota

"Kill Me" Stand

I T WAS OCTOBER 2003 AND ALL MY THOUGHTS were on deer hunting and making my twenty-fifth stand! My two sons and a nephew were along to help make the stand. I had picked a spot that would be great for seeing deer. There were multiple crossings, and other deer had been shot in the area. I had chosen a group of six oaks clumped together. That clump was on an old logging trail that meandered over to my uncle's property and had been there for over fifty years. Back when I was the age of my helpers, I would drive tractors over to my uncle's farm to swap implements with him as he was a city person who wanted to be a farmer. Those oaks were still there and were approaching fifty feet in height. The problem was that there were too many in the clump, which made it impossible to see the trail that was sure to have a trophy buck crossing it. As my young sons and their cousin helped, we added a ladder. I cut down a nice-size limb and ripped it into a two-by-six for a main bottom support. One end was fastened with nails and the other end was slotted to allow for the two trees to gently sway in the wind. After I had picked a height of about nine feet up, I decided that one of the trees just had to go. I still wanted the tree base but not the upper portion. As I stood there doing a balancing act on my homemade two-by-six, I told my helpers how dangerous this was as I had seen many trees split half way through, and I could be shaken off. Needless to say, my mind was clouded by the cold, crisp morning and the thoughts of a thirty-pointer. As I did my balancing act and began to cut through the thirty-inch-around oak, my previous words of wisdom (which I earnestly delivered to my helpers but did not listen to myself) started to come true. I watched it happen in slow motion. The tree began to split, just as I had warned. The crack shot upward and not down as I had predicted, and it went about eight feet higher han my precarious perch. It broke off the foliage portion of the tree, which hit the ground, sending the now cut end direction

44

at me a perilous speed and with accurate precision at my collar bone. When I was younger I was always trying to do flips. That day I finally succeeded, but when they told me how many I did, I was amazed even if I was in such pain. There must have been some-luck, hunting angels, or my cat-like reflexes helping out because I didn't die. As the trunk hit me, it also hit another tree, which absorbed most of the impact. The deflection off the other tree sent the now hostile tree in a direction other then the killing one it had in mind.

When I woke up, I was on my back, the saw was still running, and two of the boys were crying. My first words (at least the ones I remember) were faint, and I had to make two attempts to be heard. "Ssshu off the aw." Then I took a breath and whispered it with a little more authority. "Shut off the saw." The dang thing was still running and the chain was still moving. The boys finally moved into action once they realized that they were not going to inherit the hunting land just yet.

All I remember is the tree (larger than life) coming at me and then the softest bed ever in my life. The bed was damp molding leaves but they felt like heaven. There was a slight memory also of gently being laid down.

You are probably thinking, "What a dummy," but please remember how thoughts can get clouded this time of year, and daydreams of the Big Buck can override caution. That it overrode the caution spewing from my very mouth at the time is . . . okay, a little over the top, but it did.

So, I lived to hunt another day and thank God many more also. The stand was finished and in time for hunting season. I was banged and bruised and maybe a little wiser, at least as far as the resilience of oaks goes. The stand has produced some nice bucks over the years, but we are still waiting for the Big One.

By the way, we now have thirty-eight stands on our properties, and I am living proof that not all dumb people get culled from the herd. I plead temporary insanity caused by cold crisp mornings and the thoughts of the hunt to come. I hope that others will read this and keep their thoughts about them while they get ready for their hunts.

Life is great.

Brad Hagman
Foley, Minnesota

A Deer Story
That Stands to Rhyme

It was another deer hunting season—no snow on the ground—
The squirrels busy gathering acorns and running around.
No sight yet of a deer, but soon the does will kick it in gear.
Not to mention thee "ol' lucky" tree stand from years gone by
It's seen better days and it's not going to last.
So, with all of this on my mind,
I readjust myself on my bucket and look at the time.
I've spotted a chipmunk in the light, drizzling rain
The aroma of my coffee with cream, was his gain.
He raced up my rickety old tree stand, found his way through.
At that particular time, the excitement really grew.
I was annoyed greatly, by this (soon to be) cute little guy
Who didn't appear to be the least bit shy.
I tipped my full cup of coffee over on the ground,

In hopes to keep him busy and happy and not set up an alarm.
Exiting one of the openings under the carpet floor,
My attention now is drawn to the leaves stirring from the north.
Antlers finally come into my view.
Eyes start watering, heart racing too!
With all the racket that was just being made,
The thoughts of the rodent situation fades.
I slowly bring up my gun and hold it very still
Then let loose with a deafening blast.
The eight-point buck went down and my tag was filled.
Thank goodness for the many memories—
That darned old tree stand between those birch trunks.
By the way—Where the heck is that *blankety* chipmunk?

Jane Debner
St. Bonifacius

DISRUPTIVE PORCUPINE

I T'S SUNDAY MORNING, THE SECOND DAY of the deer hunting season in the Bemidji, Minnesota, area. I have been sitting in my stand since daybreak and have not seen a deer, so I'm heading back to my pickup truck. This is where I meet up with my hunting partners for a quick lunch and a few stories.

After my short break, I go back to my stand for the evening hunt. When I arrived there, I took off my fanny pack, which I carried my supplies in and left it on the ground under my stand. Then I climbed up into the stand and began the afternoon wait.

At 4:00 p.m. I heard something walking toward me from behind the tree. As I slowly turned with the hopes of seeing a deer, I got quite a surprise when I saw a porcupine ambling my way. It just kept coming until it was right under my stand, at which time it stepped on, investigated, then started chewing on the strap of my fanny pack. I could not believe what I was seeing and could not believe the dilemma this porcupine had put me in. I didn't want the porcupine to chew up my fanny pack, but I also didn't want to move or make noise to disrupt my possibility of getting a deer. But the spiny animal wasn't moving and seemed to be getting into his destructive munching.

I decided to drop one of my gloves straight down on him, startle him away from my stuff and still be able to hunt. The glove bounced off him, but the porcupine just kept on chewing on the strap of my fanny pack. When I realized I was spending more time watching the big rodent and not the woods for deer, and getting mad about the whole thing, I decided to climb down from the stand and scare off the animal. I did, but it took threatening him with a stick before the porcupine decided to move on and ambled off into the woods.

After settling back in my stand, I thought for sure I'd just disrupted the area, let every deer in the woods know where I was, and had just ruined my day's hunt. But those thoughts didn't last long.

Twenty minutes later, I saw movement through the trees way ahead of me. As the noise got closer I made out a huge buck. It had just come over the ridge and was heading my way. I waited for the right shot and dropped the ten-pointer neatly.

Considering my thoughts just moments before, that was not a bad ending to an event that started with a disruptive porcupine.

Steven Zacharias
Fridley

First Deer Hunt – 1966

For years I spent each weekend of pheasant season hunting ringnecks. Then it became harder and harder to have any luck, mainly because of the loss of habitat. Then a friend offered me the chance to go deer hunting. I knew nothing about the fine points of hunting deer but decided to give it a try. After all, pheasant hunting wasn't what it once was.

The only gun I had that I could use was a Japanese rifle given to me by a cousin and manufactured close to the end of World War II. I took it to a gunsmith, who took the bayonet off, put a bolt through the stock in order to hold it together and fixed me up with a box of shells. It was a right-handed rifle with a peep sight. I am left-handed. Still, I didn't want to invest in deer hunting equipment until I decided if I like it and would continue hunting deer.

I wore a pair of flight boots given to me by another cousin and a pair of flight pants. These weren't made for walking but rather for flyers who flew or rode in the World War II bombers six miles up and in temperatures that would drop to fifty below zero. For a coat I selected a parka I got from my brother who had been in the navy. Needless to say I was a sorry sight!

I went to a shooting range with a cousin to "zero in" the gun. We were shooting from a railroad boxcar, and the boom was frightening. I wasn't sure I was going to like this. When I attempted to pull off the second shot, I had trouble. I squeezed the trigger, but it soon became harder to pull, so I assumed the safety was on. It wasn't. I laid the gun on the table and took hold of the safety bolt and was going to push it in and turn the safe to on. As I started to push the bolt in, the gun fired, and the recoil about tore my thumb off. Needless to say this made me leery of the gun. Still, I thought I should give this sport a bit more of a try.

We approached the deer hunting area late at night and set up the tent camper. That night it got down to thirteen below zero, which was a record low for the opening of deer season. I had a catalytic heater, but was still freezing. I set the thermometer one foot away to check the temperature. By morning it showed ten above zero. I was inside two sleeping bags and was warm as toast but the other two people with me froze most of the night.

We awoke at an ungodly hour that would have seen pheasants still in dreamland, had a bit to eat, dressed and were ready to hit the trail. I had never been in this area before. Bob took me under his wing. I followed behind him as we marched forward. I have short legs, and, with the way I was dressed, I soon began to perspire, and my glasses fogged up. I couldn't see, so I just followed Bob's noise as he crashed through the brush.

Finally he stopped and said his stand was about a block to the left. He advised me to continue forward for a while and then climb a tree. I had no concept of distance. By now there was beginning to be a glow in the east. I walked on a ways, then picked out a tree to climb. Dressed as I was climbing was quite the task. I struggled getting up that tree, and it had looked like an easy climb. Then I had to wait. Finally it was light, but the cold began to seep in, even through my heavy layers. In order to stay warm, I would climb up and down my tree.

I was told to come down after a couple of hours and make a circle to Bob's stand. I circled and circled and found myself back on the main trail. Not where I was supposed to be maybe, but I wasn't lost. Finally I was able to find the camper. I finally got to Bob's stand about noon.

That night as we recapped the hunt, I was asked what I thought of deer hunting. How could I answer? I'd nearly frozen to death and, not only hadn't I seen a deer, I hadn't even see a bird.

The next morning the weather had warmed up considerably. I followed Bob to his deer stand, which was a large pine tree but had branches like a ladder. Bob said to go ahead for several blocks and stand by a tree and keep my eyes open and be quiet and motionless.

Again I was instructed to come back to Bob's stand after several hours. So, off I went again and waited and tried to watch. Nada.

When I got to Bob's stand several hours later, he said to climb up the pine tree stand and he would make a loop around and come back. I was, for all intents and purposes, like a son to him. He instructed me not to make quick movements and minimize any noise. The sun was out and I was enjoying the hunt. After an hour, I saw a coyote. I put my peep sights on it but decided not to pull the trigger. I was afraid Bob would criticize me for scaring deer away. I was as motionless as I could be, only turning my head like radar. I started to turn my head back when I heard a limb snap. As I turned in the direction of the snap, I saw an eight-point buck emerge from a grove of popple trees that shined like birch trees. My heart started to pound, and I was sure the deer could hear me. I had been instructed where to shoot if I saw a deer, but as the buck came slowly toward me, I wasn't sure how to shoot for the heart. I managed to get my gloves off and the gun off safe. The buck would walk forward a bit, then

The Baerts - forty-four years later. Kneeling: Ron and Jeff; standing: Quentin, Tyler, Desiree, Samantha, and Tim.

stop and look around and then proceed towards me again. I was waiting for it to go sideways so his heart would be exposed. It now was about twenty feet away when it went to the right behind another pine tree. I was thinking what Bob would say if it continued going away and I did nothing. "It was right in front of you and you didn't shoot!" But the deer, instead of going away, turned back and was now directly below me about eight feet from the tree. Again I couldn't get a side shot, all I could see was the top of the deer. Just as it started to go pass me, I pulled the trigger. The woods boomed, and the deer took off like a locomotive through the brush. In some ways the thought of trailing the deer seemed like fun, but I could imagine Bob saying, "The deer was right below you and you missed!" I attempted to eject the spent shell and put in a loaded shell, but I was having trouble getting the new shell into the barrel. I could see the deer fleeing. I looked back at the gun. Finally I got the shell in and was going to aim and fire a second shot, when I saw the deer slow down, stop, shake his leg and topple over. The bullet actually had gone right through his heart. I had no idea a deer could run seventy-five yards with a bullet hole through the heart.

Bob had told me to stay in the stand for five to ten minutes and keep an eye on the deer and also an eye out for other deer. It was only a minute or so, and Bob yelled out to stay in the stand, that he would be there in a few minutes. He was so glad I got the deer. Again I was like his son.

That night back in camp, the other hunter who had been hunting with Bob for four to five years and had never even seen a deer and had all the hunting equipment you could only dream about said somewhat tongue in cheek, "Congratulations!" He must have been green with envy. Here I was the most inexperienced deer hunter imaginable and a deer almost climbed the tree I was in. What beginner's luck!

Ron Baert
St. Cloud

BUCK SURPRISE

WHILE SITTING ON A CAMP STOOL on a little hill in an open area that was recently clear-cut of timber I was looking for a deer, hoping for a buck. That morning we had a fresh two inches of snow on the ground that had fallen during the night. First light was beautiful, very quiet and peaceful on the deer stand. From a short distance to my north, the stillness was broken by a single gunshot. Thinking that maybe someone had taken a shot at a deer, I was at full alert. If the hunter had missed that could mean a deer coming my way. About fifteen minutes after I heard that shot, I got this funny feeling that someone was looking at me. I glanced to the north. From under a pine bough I could see a deer head, and the animal was looking at me.

I slowly picked up my rifle, aimed for that deer head because that's all I could see. I wasn't sure if the deer's body in the brush was going to the left or to the right. I squeezed off a round, and the deer bolted out from the pine tree running straight away from me.

I had only two shots left in the rifle. I shot the next round at the deer and saw the dust fly up behind the deer. I then knew that I was shooting low, and my final shot had to lead the deer, which I did. I pulled the trigger, and the buck dropped on the spot. The deer was about seventy-five yards away.

I went directly to the deer to dress it out. The first thing that I do when I dress out a buck is put the deer on its back, than cut off his testicles before I insert the knife into its stomach. I really got the shock of my life when I went to cut off the testicles. There weren't any testicles there! Instead I saw just some blood coming out of a wound in this location. I then thought that the shot I heard earlier could have been a hunter jumping this deer, getting a quick shot at it while it was running away from him.

I dressed out the deer and dragged it to my stand location. After about fifteen to twenty minutes back on my stand, here come two hunters tracking blood in the fresh fallen snow. They were so intent on tracking the blood trail, they didn't even see me sitting on my stand. I yelled, "Hey!"

That startled them, and they said, "Did you see a deer come by this way?"

I said, "Yes, I did and I shot him. He's lying right here beside me."

"Can we see him?"

I said sure. When they looked at this nice six-point buck, I told them what I had discovered. "Whoever shot at this buck shot a little low. The testicles were shot off." I showed them.

Those were two very surprised hunters, just as I had been. What a surprise indeed! And that was a first for me as well.

Vincent Shallbetter
Mora, Minnesota

THE HILTON

THE ORIGIN OF THE HILTON BEGAN over forty years ago when I first met Tom and he gave me a part time job while I was attending college. We quickly established a friendship that has lasted and grown for all of these forty-plus years. He took this young southwestern Minnesotan under his wing. I only knew how to shoot pheasants and fish for bullheads. He taught me how to really fish and hunt. We ice fished in the winter, fished in his boat in the summer, then hunted ducks, geese, and deer in the fall. The fishing and hunting started in Minnesota, but gradually spread into Canada. We went several times to Saskatchewan duck and goose hunting in the 1970s. I can't count how many times we have gone fishing in Canada together. Many of those trips were fly-in fishing trips. Over the years, because of each of us moving and raising our own families, we drifted apart somewhat and did a lot less fishing and hunting together. We did manage to get in a few trips together, which included some pheasant hunting in South Dakota.

In August of 1996, my life changed forever. I was a passenger in a car accident that took my wife's life and left me paralyzed from the waist down. But once again there was Tom. He would visit me during my rehabilitation process, from Hennepin County Medical Center to St. Cloud Hospital to St. Benedicts Center and eventually he dove me home to Baxter, for the first time. It was such a long distance from Baxter to the St. Cloud Hospital for my Rehab and doctor visits that I decided the build a patio home in Waite Park to facilitate things better.

Tom was there immediately, encouraging me to get back to hunting and fishing. Eight months after I was out of the hospital, I was headed to Canada fishing, and four months after that pheasant hunting in South Dakota. Tom tried for several years to get me to go deer hunting with him at his farm. But I was not quite ready to take that on once again. But after several years of Tom's persistence, I decided to give it a try. The first four or five years I hunted off Tom's four-wheeler, and I actually shot a deer the first year. A couple of the years were pretty cold, so I bought a ground blind and heater. That was quite a step up from sitting on the four-wheeler all day. I just about always saw a deer or two, but it was always hard to get a good shot at them. Although, one year I did get a descent shot and got one. I guess that I hunted in my ground blind for three or four years. But each year when Tom, Judd, Lee, and I got together during our "After the Hunt Cocktail Hour," Tom would say that he was going to find a way to build a box stand that I could hunt out of. He wanted me to be up in the air, so I could see the deer better. Then, in September of 2008, I got an email with several pictures, which showed the process of my new deer stand being built. There was Tom, his son Judd, and my other hunting buddy, Lee, erecting my new stand. It was amazing! We weren't too optimistic about my success the first year because the deer

stand wasn't finished until mid-October. It might be too soon for the deer to settle down from all the commotion.

But late on the second afternoon I saw a deer and was able to harvest it. That was an unbelievable experience for me. This last year, we were limited to one antlerless deer apiece, so we were quite selective. It was a good year for me seeing deer. I saw six and had four small ones in front of me, about twenty yards away, at one time. I passed on them so that they could grow bigger next year. I have never hunted just for the meat, rather for the enjoyment of being with my hunting friends. We ended up with enough venison for the four of us, anyway. I can't think of anything better then to spend time with your friend hunting and socializing afterwards and telling deer stories.

There is another person who requires a lot of my thanks. That is Tom's wife, Karen. Every year she helps us out with processing the deer and making us nice warm meals after the hunt. Her help is immensely appreciated, by me.

Words will never express my friendship with Tom and my tremendous gratitude for all that he has done for me, over the years. And "The Hilton" (my deer stand) is just another example of what an amazing person he is. All I can say is . . . Tom, thank you so much giving me back a big part of my life.

Dick Schulstad
Waite Park, Minnesota

COYOTE

How many coyotes does it take to eat one adult deer? The following is an account of what happened to me in the fall of 2007: It was a nice October day so I thought I would spend the last couple of hours of daylight in one of my many bow stands located on my farm in Sherburne County near St. Cloud. About half an hour before dark a fork-horn buck walked by on his way to feed in one of my corn food plots. I passed on him, thinking another, bigger buck might be following him. When the second buck came into view, I saw that it was another fork-horn. Needing some fresh venison for the freezer, I figured he would fit just fine. (For all you QDM folks out there, passing a

small buck in this county means passing him to the neighbor to shoot.) When this second deer reached my shooting lane, he paused before stepping out into the field. I came to full draw and released my arrow.

The solid thunk of the arrow told me I had a good hit. He spun around and made a death charge back the way he had come. I thought I heard him crash about seventy-five yards behind me. With very little daylight

left, and my inability to see a blood trail (I'm red-green color blind), I elected not to go and look for him until I could get my son (the best blood tracker I've ever seen) to help me. Shortly after dark my son, my wife, and I went into the woods, armed with flashlights, to find my deer. Upon showing them where I hit the deer and where he ran, we began our search. After two hours, not so much as a trace of blood was to be found—no arrow, no hair, nothing. We were left with combing the woods in the area where I thought he fell. By 10:00 p.m., our flashlights were dead and we were tired, so we gave up for the night thinking we would resume the search in the morning with good daylight. After a restless night, my wife and I took up the chase at daybreak. Upon entering the woods and nearing the spot where I thought he should be, I could smell fresh blood. (I may be color blind, but I have an excellent sense of smell). We found what was left of my deer spread over an area about the size of a living room. The sight was unbelievable. There were no guts and no hide, just a totally dismembered deer carcass, which I later reconstructed on my lawn. All of this happened in an eight-hour time frame. I've seen coyotes eat out a hind quarter overnight, but never eat a whole deer—including the guts and hide. How many coyotes does it take to do that? Do you think we have a predator problem? I do.

Tom Machula
Sauk Rapids

Judd and Tom.

BONNIE'S STAND

FIFTEEN YEARS AGO, MY WIFE, Bonnie, was the first one to hunt from this stand. A few years later, my hunting partner, Donnie, suggested we change the name to Donnie's Stand. It didn't stick. Bonnie's stand is not unusual, only four feet by four feet, and it's not my number one stand. It does keep me warm during muzzleloader season when the temperatures can drop to zero. Between muzzleloader and rifle season, I spend about fifty to sixty hours in Bonnie's Stand.

Dave.

The biggest buck to date shot out of Bonnie's Stand was a 151-inch, fourteen-pointer. It was the last Saturday of muzzleloader season in 2008, and I was on call for Center Point Energy, and, of course, I got called out. I was anxious to hunt that evening and worked fast to get the job done so I could get out to my stand, hoping not to get called out again. It had been two nights earlier that I had seen a good buck out of Bonnie's Stand right at dark. But with no binoculars or scope on the muzzleloader, I was not able to see if he was big enough. All I knew was that he was nice, and I wanted to see him again. I finished my job and was in

Bonnie's Stand by three that afternoon. The stand sits over a purple-top turnip food plot to the north and has good deer bedding locations to the west. I had does come in to the turnips all season. I planted the turnips for the does and had left them alone in hopes a mature buck would step out of the bedding area during shooting hours and check out the does.

At about 4:15 p.m. and about 100 yards away, the drop-tine buck stepped out of the woods to check out the does in the food plot. With one shot in the chest, he made three bounds away, then fell. When I went to get the truck, the temperature read zero degrees. Without the heater in the stand, it would have been a tough, cold hunt. The buck scored 151 inches. I had him aged from a tooth, and the was four and one-half years old. I had a camera watching over the plot since June and never had a picture of him. He was standing about twenty yards from the camera when I shot him.

David Edblad
Cambridge, Minnesota

This is Cliffy Edblad on his first deer hunt inside Bonnie's stand. He was five years old at the time. He saw a doe and a fawn that night. Cliffy shows great potential for a future deer hunter.

IS IT? OR ISN'T IT?

Not sure it is a "buck," is what I told my uncle that afternoon when I came up to his house. Of course it was a buck, but was it a *legal* buck? I was fourteen or fifteen and I was still hunting. (I'm really glad they gave a name to my inability to sit in a stand for too long) I was walking/hunting about three miles from our farm on my way to my uncle's place. I had planned to take most of the afternoon getting there and then get into my favorite stand for the evening hunt. It was my only stand and had proven to produce the largest buck I have ever gotten. I was almost to my uncle's when, ahead of me, a deer crossed my path. It was headed south towards the river, so I quickly assessed the wind direction and moved southward from where I was in anticipation of cutting off the deer by getting ahead of it. I caught sight of it after I had moved into the woods, and it was a small buck. I quickened my pace and crossed the ditch I had been paralleling for a quarter mile. This looked like the spot for an ambush, so I stood motionless and waited. I could see the logging road we made through the woods and, back in an L shape was some good shooting lanes. Now this was hunting I thought. I waited for only a couple minutes when I saw a deer coming from the south heading north. The deer was wet as if it had just crossed the river.

This was odd as the one I was following was heading *towards* the river. The shot was good, so I took it. It was then as I was dressing the deer that I was wondering if it was a legal buck as his two antlers were very short. I pulled out my knife and used it as a measuring device and headed up to my uncle's. Upon getting there, he asked me if I had shot a buck. I said, "Well that depends. Give me a tape measure." After I measured my knife, I told him, "Yep, it's a buck by half an inch!" There have been many a young buck that has fallen to my gun but I learned shortly that this was not the sport I wanted. These bucks were dumb to the ways of hunting. It was the old ones I wanted, ones that required more expertise to bag. I believe I had sighted two bucks that day. I think I did get around the one I saw first and there was no time for him to make it to the river, go swimming and then back to me. Shooting the second tipped off the first deer to hightail it. I didn't make it to the stand that day, but it turned out well anyway.

Brad Hagman
Foley, Minnesota

GOING GREEN
THE BUCK SHACK

ONCE UPON A TIME . . . This is the story of how a once discarded tent camper transformed from a junkyard ornament, then referred to as a "popcorn wagon," to a state-of-the-art hunting blind on wheels known as the "Buck Shack.

At last, the search was over. Off in the distance, surrounded by burdocks and overgrown by other weeds, sat an old tent camper on a vacant farm lot in southeastern Minnesota. Although it had seen better days in the campground, the old trailer had a hidden potential that only a handyman could recognize—a vision of a heated portable hunting blind on wheels!

It wasn't until a week later that I noticed some activity at the vacant farm. The perfect opportunity to ask about the old camper was in front of me.

I pulled in for a friendly visit with the owner over a couple of ice cold beers. Before long, the conversation turned to permission to deer hunt on the land and what the owner intended to do with the old camper. It turned out that someone else had envisioned the camper as an ice shack, and they had gone as far as removing the entire inside of the camper but couldn't removed the wheels to replace the tires. So, I was offered the camper for a price I could "never" turn down— Free!

I knew we could handle the construction portion of the project, but in its junkyard condition, the hard part would be convincing my lovely and understanding wife, now known as Lu, to allow me to bring this treasure into the driveway. As expected, my vision was not warmly welcomed as a permanent item for her yard. I explained that the stay would be only temporary. Lu's next question was about the cost of this undertaking. I said, "Nuthin', honey. It was free."

This was in May. By September I had still not gotten around to actually picking the camper up. Then my son Bill and I realized that hunting season was right around the corner. Time for some action!

Getting the camper out of its resting place was no easy task. The tires needed to be replaced before it could tackle the open road. After bringing out a skidloader, impact gun, sockets, and extension cords, my son fought with the trailer long enough to realize that the wheel studs were left handed. Then wheel removal was easier.

The tire shop was next. We needed to get the wheels and tires into road-worthy condition. That part of the job went well.

It was time to pull the camper home. With a roll of her eyes, Lu expressed how nice it looked at that point.

A good pressure washing helped to removed the years of dirt and rust that had built up on the exterior, and water running inside it helped to chase out the mice.

We washed the camper again with a bleach solution, and then aired it out. Now she was as clean as possible.

Ben and the antlers of many bucks.

It was October, time to start with the construction, but more materials were needed. Left over barn steel, steel studs, some plywood and plexiglass were found at a great price, my kind of price—again free! An old sliding rear window from a pickup truck made the perfect front shooting window. Windows were framed and the walls were reinforced and insulated. The recycling center had plenty of brown, tan, and green paint to donate to my cause.

About 1:00 a.m., with slug season just six days away, and I was having trouble sleeping. I figured we might as well get up and test my artistic abilities with that free paint and a brush.

My lovely and understanding bride came out to the shop about 9:30 that morning, and Lu exclaimed, "Who are you, some type of reincarnated Van Gough?"

I think Lu was actually impressed! Corn painted on the brown steel, woods camo on the white steel—what a masterpiece! All of a sudden, Lu didn't care if it sat right in the driveway—a trophy of the ingenuity and craftsmanship of her beloved husband. The in-

Chloe Rose.

side was also finished. Complete with a wood stove, deer horns to hang coats and backpacks from, and a urinal. It even had the seal of approval from my five-year-old granddaughter, Chloe Rose. She said, "Grandma, we could live in here forever!"

Now, there were skeptics about his blind on wheels. They said, "The deer will need plenty of time to get used to it," and "The smell of fresh paint and wood smoke will keep them away."

Regardless of the criticism, we embarked on the maiden voyage out to Kent's waterway. I had a feeling the deer wouldn't be spooked by the blind. After all, how many times have hunters parked their trucks and walked away, then turned around to see a buck standing right next to the trucks?

The day after the ex-camper was parked in the waterway, Kent witnessed two does right beside it. The first test had been passed. "What about the wood smoke issue?" Kent said. I replied, "The smoke will bring the deer in like they were tied to a string."

December 1, muzzleloader season was upon us when I first enjoyed the comfort of this heated hunting blind. I had just re-loaded the wood stove when I looked up and, out of the truck window, saw a big deer through the apple trees. Large doe per-haps? Basket-rack buck maybe? Fieldglasses up. Oh, no, this was a shooter buck! My blood pressure and heart rate started climbing. Would I have the chance to redeem myself for the big buck I missed during slug season?

Past the apple trees, through the pines and into the walnut trees he ran. I took some deep breaths to try to calm down, and took the best shot I could with the ol' smoke stick.

As the smoke cleared from the big *boom* of the muzzle-loader, I saw the buck, tail straight in the air, running into the thick woods. Had I hit him? Had I missed? Although I knew I had to stay put for a while, my mind was racing, hands shaking. "Oh, that's right. Time to reload." After reloading, I ran the shot over and over in my mind.

After a short while, I went out to the spot and found a lot of dark-red blood. Pinker blood would have been a lot better sign, it still looked like a good hit. I decided I better give the deer a bit more time to lay down.

But, wait! I was supposed to go shopping with Lu today. I quick phone call to Lu to tell her of my luck, and I felt better. After all, I had been hunting a lifetime to get a buck like this one! Lu said, "Good luck, and I hope you find him. Keep me informed. I said she was lovely and understanding.

A couple of hours passed, and it was back to the blood trail, lots of blood everywhere. It looked like he might of fallen right here. I followed a very good blood trail up through the woods, but then I saw a deer bouncing up and out of the woods. "Oh, great! I blew it. I didn't give him enough time, and now he's gone."

Minutes later, dogs began barking nearby, and I heard a few shots. I thought, "Now what?" So I followed the blood trail to the neighbor's land. It still looked like a good hit.

It was time to head back to the truck and get permission from the neighbors to continue on the trail. So I drove over to the area where I heard the dogs and the shots. "After all," I told myself, "just maybe the neighbors will at least let me take a picture of the buck I just chased to them."

But nobody was hunting over there. So I was allowed to enter their property to track my buck. But first I needed to back-track the blood trail. In my haste, I never found the spot where he was lying down. After back-tracking to the area where the deer jumped up, I discovered he never did lie down in the woods. Now that got my heart pumping again.

Four hours passed since I took that first shot. I started tracking the deer into the tall grass, still following a lot of blood. About forty feet into the grass, I saw where he had lain down. He had gotten up and gone twenty-five feet further, then lay down again. Then I couldn't tell which way he went. I couldn't find any more blood.

I walked in circles for a while, looking everywhere. I decided I needed some help. So I called my son, but got no answer. He was home sick with the flu. I kept looking. While I was checking a mowed path for fresh tracks on the other side of the field, my son called back. At the sound of the ring, the buck suddenly jumped up. I threw down the phone and shot again at the buck of a lifetime. He looked huge running straight away from me!

I missed. Time to load up the "smoke pole" one more time. Then I caught sight of him. He was standing on the edge of the woods. All I could see were the antlers above the grass. It was time to close the distance.

As I began my way through the grass, I heard a crash in the woods. It sounded as if he had fallen down. I ran to the edge of the woods and took another shot. I hit him that time, and he went about another twenty yards. There he finally lay down for the last time.

This buck was over 200 pounds, twenty and one-half inches wide, with nine points and grossed 150 inches. I have hunted deer for forty years, and enjoyed every hunt. This year just turned out to be one of the best!

So that's the story of how this hunting blind that used to be a tent camper got used as the Buck Shack. Not only did I have good luck, my son Bill, who had helped build the Buck Shack, got a 130-inch buck, and Kent, who donated the wood stove, got a 150-inch buck in Canada this year.

The Buck Shack appeared to be lucky for all who had a hand in bringing the junkyard ornament back to life.

In the years to come, as we warmed our hands over the wood stove, I hope that those who join me in the Buck Shack will enjoy hearing this story as much as I enjoyed telling it.

But most of all, I look forward to sharing the hunting blind with my grandchildren, Ben and Chloe, as they come of age to hunt with their dad, Bill, and their Grampa Buck.

We hope you enjoyed our story about the Buck Shack. There were two more nice mature does taken using the blind. And at least a dozen more deer were passed up. Even the skeptics are enjoying the comfort of the Buck Shack with confidence that it wasn't chasing the deer away. The end (well, not really).
Mark "Buck" Schreader
Pine Island, Minnesota

IS IT DEAD?

M Y YOUNGER BROTHER, KEN, WAS just out of the Army one year as deer hunting was fast approaching. While talking to him, he stated that he'd like to go deer hunting with me and my hunting pals. He knew how to handle a weapon from his experiences in the Army. We went out to the gun range to fire a few rounds and all things looked great. The night before opening day at deer camp, in the cabin we rented for deer season, the stories were really flying. Brother Ken was taking them all in. One of the guys told the story where he shot a deer, came up to it thinking that this deer was dead and all of sudden the deer jumped up and kicked him severely with his very sharp hoofs. We told Ken, if he shoots a deer, to come up to it and put a final round into its head to make sure he was dead and not playing possum.

The next morning, I placed Ken on the south end of a local lake called Doe Lake. About 500 yards to the north was where my stand was located. We used army camp stools for our deer stand, and they worked great. The sun was just rising, and it was ten degrees below zero, very cold. I poured out a cup of coffee from my thermos, set it on the ground to cool, not realizing the steam from that cup of coffee was steaming up the scope on my rifle. All of a sudden, I heard a deer walking down the draw in front of me. I saw the deer, carefully picked up my rifle, sighted into my scope to get a bead on this deer, but something was wrong. The scope was all fogged up. Before I realized just what happened, the sound of this deer was out of sight. The good news was that this deer was walking south towards my brother. I thought, maybe, just maybe, Ken could get a shot at this deer if it kept walking south towards my brother. About half an hour later I heard a gunshot from the south. Then I heard a second shot and then a third. There was quite a gap, five to ten minutes, and then another shot (the fourth) then another and another and yet one more. That was seven shots. I was hoping all this shooting came from where my brother was. But the shooting wasn't over yet. I counted nine more shots from that area. I thought, *My goodness, Ken's shooting at a whole herd of deer!* The total amounts of shots fired was sixteen.

When it got quiet at last, I walked to Ken's stand and there was only one deer lying dead. I asked Ken why so many shots. He said he heard the stories in deer camp last night and he didn't want to get kicked, so after he had the deer down, he pulled his sidearm (a .45) and shot nine shots into the head to make sure the deer was dead, well, I guess so! Yup, that deer wasn't going to kick anyone. Nope, not ever.

Vince Shallbetter
Mora

Old Geezers' Final Stand

LOOKING BACK OVER THE YEARS, I've built many, many deer stands throughout the state of Minnesota. I've been deer hunting for over fifty years as well as my deer-hunting partner, "Big Pete," and we're now both in our seventies, but the deer hunting spirit still lives within us.

Four years ago, while driving around looking for a new spot to hunt deer near our area, Big Pete suggested that we drive to his son's property south of Aitkin, Minnesota. He has some wooded acres that attract deer. We could take a couple lawn chairs, walk into the woods to this nice ridge that would give us an advantage point to look for deer and maybe give us a chance at shooting one. We did just that.

Big Pete's knees aren't the best, so he couldn't walk too far, but he only had to walk twenty-five or thirty yards to that ridge to set up his lawn chair. I continued another sixty to seventy-five yards further down that same ridge and set up my lawn chair. While walk-

ing to my location, I notice a lot of deer sign—tracks and drop-pings—so I knew that many deer dwelled in this area. I had hope of seeing a deer to shoot at. After about only one hour, as so often happens while sitting in the woods on a deer stand or stump, we both got cold. It was late November, a rather chilly day and there was a wind. We ended the deer hunt for the day without seeing any deer.

After the two of us were out of the woods and starting to warm up, Big Pete said to me, "I really like those woods and that ridge for hunting deer. I got this idea while sitting there looking for deer. Wouldn't it be nice to build a permanent deer stand on that ridge deeper in the woods and up high so we'd have a real advantage point? We could enclose the stand, put some heat in it."

Vince   Pete

"What a great idea," I said. "Let's do it."

After choosing a good location and checking with Big Pete's son for permission to do so, we agreed on the size and what materials to use. We made blue prints that winter and started looking for building material and talked about how we would share the expenses. We agreed on a clean fifty-fifty.

That next fall we had gathered up materials to build our deer stand which included six four-by-four treated wood posts, eight feet long. The plan was to put at least one foot into the ground and cement them in for stability. We kept running into either rocks or roots of trees while digging our holes for the posts, so that part of the job was a bit of a challenge. Completed, that left one foot of our posts in the ground, giving us a height of seven feet. We were told to anchor these posts in the ground, and had bought some Sacrete. We poured that into the holes without adding any water because the moisture from the ground would be sucked into the Sacrete and make the cement. The following week when we went out to the deer stand the posts were as solid as a rock, mission done. We took Big Pete's four-wheeler, along with a old boat trailer of mine, attached a four-by-eight piece of plywood for the base to haul all the material to the building site, along with Big Pete's generator for power. Construction began.

Our plans were to build an eight-by-eight structure with a four-by-eight deck along with a staircase and two hand rails. The project was started in August 2007. Big Pete had one knee replaced in 2006 and the second replaced the summer of 2007 thinking that all would be healed by deer hunting season. Walking 125 yards from the truck to the deer stand wasn't in the cards for him. He rode his four-wheeler to the stand. The staircase with two hand rails allowed him to climb into our deer stand.

Included in the deer stand, we installed three double glass sliding windows, one each on three sides for a wide vantage and good shooting options. Inside the deer stand, we brought two swivel chairs with arm rests and high backs that could tilt back. They had rollers for easy mobility around inside the deer stand. We also brought a small folding table for the deer stand that we could put our lunch on and a place to play a game of cribbage from time to time. We installed a metal cabinet on the wall to store different items like binoculars, ear muffs, Kleenex, our cribbage board and cards. Under the floor we built a stand to put our twenty-pound propane tank and drilled a hole into the three-quarter-inch floor to run the hose to our propane heater in the deer stand. "Voila!" We had heat in our deer stand.

We covered the ceiling with a clear plastic tarp, then put cardboard on top of that for a vapor barrier to help keep the heat in our deer stand. It worked like a charm.

While building this deer stand, Big Pete's son, Kevin a carpenter by trade, helped us with the construction. Once Big Pete and I had the floor in place and the structure in place, Kevin would get up on the floor and say to Big Pete and me, "I'll give you guys the measurements, you cut the wood, hand it up to me, and I'll pound the nails." What a blessing to have Kevin help us, including putting up the roof. The roof overhangs the building, was covered with tar paper and roll roofing, to keep the rain and snow flowing to the ground instead of into the deer stand.

November 2007, the deer stand was ready to use for deer hunting for the first time. Three weekends, we sat there and didn't see a deer, although we knew that the deer were in those woods somewhere. We figured that the deer were getting used to this new structure in their woods where they lived.

November 2008, our second year in this deer stand was different. Opening weekend a very nice mature doe came running by the deer stand on the south side.

Later that afternoon, a nice yearling deer walked by the north side of the deer stand. 1 looked through the binoculars and saw no antlers. We were at a area where only bucks could be taken this year. To us we were happy just to see deer from our newly built deer stand. The following weekend, the second weekend of the season, on a late Saturday morning, Big Pete all of a sudden said to me, "I think 1 see a deer to the west of the deer stand." It was down one of the four shooting lanes we'd opened up. Again, I grabbed the binoculars and looked in the direction he was indicating and lo and behold there was a deer, a nice eight-point buck at that. 1 couldn't believe it. 1 turned to Big Pete and said, "Yes, it's a deer and yes, it's a buck, a eight-pointer. I grabbed my ear muffs and put them on. Big Pete did the same thing. I took my Remington level-action 30/30 loaded, slid open the west window, and put that eight-point buck into the cross hairs. After the third shot, the buck jumped up in the air and kicked like a mule. I knew I hit him. He ran down a hill, stood there a moment, then all I could see of him was his tail flagging as he disappeared. I thought he'd be lying on the ground when I got there, but all I could find was a pool of blood, where he had been standing flagging. I looked all over and could not find any more blood. He got away. That was really exciting and to me a success just to see a deer and have a chance to shoot at it.

This year, 2009, I told Big Pete, "This year it's your turn to shoot and miss a deer."

Hanging on the outside wall of our deer stand is a sign that reads, "Old Geezers Final Stand." There is a yellow metal sign on a tree next our deer stand that reads "Monster Buck Crossing." The last sign was just put up this year inside our deer stand. It reads: "Good things happen to those who wait" with a photo of a large monster buck with a giant rack of horns.

We really enjoy our deer stand, and it's so nice to be able to keep warm! "Fantastic and Hallelujah!"

Vincent Shallbetter
Mora

THE HUNTING CABIN GANG

In 1994, three cousins, Neil, Fred, and Mike, and brother-in-law Dave bought 210 acres in central Wisconsin north of Prentice. Much to our delight, the neighbors and surrounding hunting groups—Buck Not Gang, Pump House Gang, K Kampa, Bear Camp—were great folks.

Our fathers, our kids, and some of our friends built a cabin with wood heat, a wood cook stove, and gas lights. We were pretty proud of our creation to say the least!

Fred's daughter Joan hunted with us a few years back. A couple of years ago, Mike met Joan as she had been hunting both

bow and gun seasons with us the last three years. She wasn't real fond of the cold or bears, so I decided to give her a box stand that I built. She feels safer, as the bears can't reach her as easily. But since she was pretty and feminine, I wanted to do something special for her. Without her knowing it, I painted her box stand camo pink. Joan called it her She-Safari Stand.

Joan said, "First came my love of being in the woods. Then came hunting. From little on, somehow trees were comforting to me. I had one particular oak tree that had the perfect sitting spot among its limbs. It has been over thirty-five years since I've sat in that tree, but it still stands, holding my memories, and I am grateful for that. My interest in hunting did not really begin until I was an adult, but, looking back, I was intrigued even as a young girl with my father's hunting stories. The few times I was brought to their hunting camp, which consisted of an old school bus, outdoor house and buck pole, I thought it was magical. I have hunted on and off over the years but never belonged to a hunting camp until the fall of 2006. My husband and three other guys have a hunting cabin up in Prentice and were gracious enough to include me. I love being up there. The simplicity is a welcomed escape from the hurried pace of daily life. Walking out into the woods in the crisp early morning air, taking in all the sounds and smells is amazing. Sitting in the tree, whether during bow or gun season, allows me time not just to maybe put down a nice deer, but also gives me time to reflect on life. It is a perfect place to play . . . right smack in the middle of God's creation. I think more people should sit in a tree! Neil and Gabe Steinagel put up my "She-Safari" stand this past fall . . . surprised me totally! I love that the stand shows my "girlie" side. Life is good when in the woods!

WE ALL GET ALONG GREAT IN OUR HUNTING CAMP. We have never had a big argument in the cabin. The closest we ever came was one night while we were playing cards. I guess we had it a little too warm. Fred came out of his "upper" bunk, sat on the couch and started to read the newspaper. His son and my son noticed sweat running down his face. They started laughing, and pretty soon we all were laughing. All except Fred. He was not happy and explained that point to us. After a few minutes, we promised not to fire up the stove so full anymore.

Actually, we had a few hunting cabin rules. One day five of us were out moving a box stand. I looked at Mike and said, "Hold still." I reached over and swiped a finger full of white foam

out of his ear. The night before we'd had apple pie with whipped cream for dessert. Gabe had looked thoughtfully at his whipped cream, then pointedly at Mike. Mike pretty much could see his mind churning and warned, "Don't even think about it." Gabe laughed, and the game was on. Over the table flew a dollop of whipped cream. Onto the floor, over the couch. Pretty soon flecks of the stuff had reached everyone in the cabin, and we all had tears in our eyes from laughing so hard. We had no rule to avoid food fights. This event was as funny as the goofy buzzing fly that the guys played fly hockey with, blowing the fly from one end of the table to the other before it got tired of us and flew off. No rule about that either.

IN 2008, DAVE'S SONS LUKE AND CODY both shot their first bucks just a couple of days apart. It was great.

Cody built his own stand in a spot he picked out by himself. In 2008, he had a nice buck sneak through, and he was getting pretty excited sitting there with his new rifle. Luke and Cody's grandfather had bought them both rifles of their choice just prior to his passing away. I'm sure he was watching as his two grandsons shot their first bucks.

Cody was so excited about his first deer, he wanted to surprise us all. So he didn't gut it as that would leave a blood trail back to camp. Instead, he dragged it over a quarter of a mile back to camp and hid it behind the trailer. After we were all back at camp, the topic of the funny marks on the logging road came up. As everyone was trying to figure

out what the marks meant and getting around to the idea that something had been dragged along the road, Cody admitted he made the tracks and proudly showed us his buck.

WE WERE ALL OUT MAKING A DRIVE, which wasn't easy in the Big Woods country. It's important not to mess up on those drives. Luke was too young to hunt, but we often took our kids out as soon as they could walk along okay. Luke wanted to post with Gabe because he was the best shot and was usually good-natured about having kids with him.

The drive was going along fine when, suddenly, Luke whispered to Gabe, "There's a deer!"

Gabe said, "Where?"

"Over there."

"I don't see it."

Luke pointed. "It's right by that tree in the tall grass."

Gabe squinted. "I still don't see it."

"All you can see is its eyes."

Finally Gabe spotted it. "I can't get a shot at it."

Luke said, "Can't you shoot it between the eyes?"

The deer was some sixty to seventy yards away. With open sights on his 300 Savage, Gabe felt a little sheepish. "Yeah, I guess I could do that." He took aim.

One shot and they had a dead deer. That was Luke's big story for the rest of the season.

IN 2007, NEIL STEINAGLE, ONE OF THE CREW, had shoulder surgery a few weeks before hunting. He couldn't shoot his rifle, but he went to the cabin with his .44 magnum. By mid-season, I just had to get into the woods. With some practice and a stick to steady his aim, he was able to hunt left handed. Although he couldn't hunt very long, he was able to go, and almost got to shoot at a nice doe. He needed to be a little faster if he was going to get his deer, though, or the deer needed to be more cooperative.

MIKE AND FRED WERE OUT BOW hunting one day. They were about 150 yards or so apart. It was time to come out of the stands one night, but, as Mike was getting his things together, he thought he heard someone, but that didn't make sense. He continued getting his stuff organized and was just about to climb down his ladder, when he heard the sound again. He stopped and listened more closely. "Holy cow," he said to himself. "That's Fred! He must be hanging from his harness."

Mike quickly jumped on his ATV and roared right over to Fred's post. He got out his little mini-flashlight. "Fred! Fred! You okay, buddy?"

Fred called back, "I am now."

Then Fred told Mike that a big sow bear and three cubs had been hanging around and wouldn't leave. The sow had been upset, chomping her teeth, and Fred was afraid she would come up the tree where he was.

Mike scanned his flashlight all around, asking where the bears were. "Oh, they ran off when your ATV came roaring in."

They sure had an exciting tale to tell back at the cabin.

Jordan and Brenna.

Gabe's five-year-old daughter Brenna had her first hunting season at the cabin. She loved it and she added extra excitement to the cabin, not to mention that we now had two "women" sticking together when we tried to tease them. Brenna even went out and sat in a box stand with her father for a little while. As our kids

Neil's outhouse. The kids and girls love it.

grow up, they all go through the lessons in gun safety and progressing till they got to the first gun season when they could hunt.

WE HAD 210 ACRES, BUT IT WAS in an L shape, one half by one mile long. Mike liked to put his stand on the outside perimeter, off the beaten path, among the trees down by the river. It could be dark, damp and spooky down there. Neil and some of the others wouldn't even go to Mike's stand unless it was a nice, sunny day.

One evening just before dark, a movement caught Mike's eye down by the river. He looked and watched. Suddenly, the hair on the back of his neck bristled. Cougar! Slipping along the river edge, the big cat was making its way right past his stand. Mike, mostly frozen in fear, held his breath and watched as a the cougar meandered away.

Later, back at the cabin, Mike related what he had seen. He ended with, "So . . . who wants to sit in my stand tomorrow?" Everyone laughed and declined.

Mike continued to hunt from that stand, but was never without his flashlight and liked to leave before daylight was entirely gone.

ABOUT EIGHT OR NINE YEARS AGO, the crew at the cabin was getting ready to do a drive, but they needed extra drivers, so Luke piped up, saying he could drive. He had passed his compass training, and the adults figured they could keep him in sight the whole time. However, we told him, if he was going to be a driver, he had to carry a gun. "Take the BB gun along," he was told. Luke thought about it, then declined because it was pretty thick in the woods.

About halfway through the drive, Luke said to Neil, "I see a deer." He pointed to where a doe was lying down right behind a brush pile. Neil asked if he could see it well, and Luke added, "Yeah. If I had that BB gun, I could shoot it in the head!"

Josh Steinagel

Left to right: Neis Steinagel, Jessie Robinson, chris Steinagel, Gabe Steinagel, Mike Steinagel, Dave Sliwickis, Fred Steinagel, with Luke Sliwickis in front.

He walked over toward the deer, and it took off. Luke yelled, "She's coming your way, Mike!" The deer got away, but the story got repeated often. Luke carried the BB gun after that.

GABE USED TO TAKE BRENNA OUT WHEN she was very young (about three) while he was tracking deer. She rode on his shoulders. By then she already understood why they gutted deer, dragged them back to camp and cut them up. Her favorite thing was to color the wrapped meat packages and put them in the upright freezer.

Kids loved to help in camp. Some of them had trouble going out alone to pee. When that happened, someone would holler, "Team pee," and a bunch of people would go along. Kids thought that was cool.

Neil Steinagle
The cabin gang
Wausaw, Wisconsin

QUICK EXIT

Back in the good ol' days, Donny, Ed and I (Joe) were hunting north of Nashwauk, hoping to have a good deer hunting time. The day before hunting, we got up there and spent the afternoon building a nice stand for Donny. That night we were joined by Norb and Stan. After supper, we talked "deer stories" and safety with guns.

At about six the next morning, we all got into a circle facing outward and had our guns pointed down. It was very still, so all we could hear was the sound of shells being loaded into the guns. All of a sudden, *ka-plow*, a gun went off. I must have jumped a foot off the ground. Then we looked around to find out what had happened. Norb, a little sheepishly, explained that he wanted to see if his gun was on safe by testing the trigger. The gun wasn't on safe.

I sure didn't want to hunt close to him that day. After that big scare, we all headed off into the woods to hunt. When Donny got to his stand, it was still dark, but, wouldn't you know, there was a stranger in the stand. Donny, being a gentleman, just walked off about a hundred feet and sat down by a tree. He was just fooling around with his gun, checking everything, when ka-boom, it went off. About then Donny was regretting getting that hair trigger setting before he got up deer hunting.

Then he heard some noise coming down his tree stand. It was the stranger coming down and leaving without saying a word. So Donny got his tree stand back anyway.

We were hunting north of Grand Rapids, between Marcell and Talmoon, with a party of eight. By 7:00 opening morning, all of us were in the woods except Melvin.

Melvin was on vacation from Seattle and was a buddy from way back. He enjoyed hunting deer years ago, but he wasn't about to get up at five in the morning. About 9:00, he got out of the shack, took a swig of eye-opener, grabbed his gun and headed down the trail. About 500 feet down the trail, he took another swig and noticed the pint was half empty. He knew that wouldn't last the day, so he went back to fill it and finally got around to leaving camp about 10:00.

A short way down the trail he heard a noise in the brush, and a spooked buck burst onto the trail and stopped. Despite having drunk enough to see two deer, Melvin took aim on one of them and fired. He chose well. The buck dropped right in its tracks.

Melvin dragged the deer back to camp and decided to hunt the trail in the other direction. Coming back to camp at noon, the group saw the gut pile on the trail and the drag trail back to camp, but no Melvin. After a quick lunch they all headed out again. But after the afternoon hunt, none of them had scored and were anxious to hear Melvin's story.

As it got dark, Melvin still wasn't back, and some of the guys took off in the truck to check the trails. About a mile from camp, they saw the dim lights of a van a little ways off the trail. They stopped to check if these people had seen a lost hunter, but they found Melvin instead.

He had met the van owner, another hunter, on the trail. The guy turned out to be a liquor salesman, and lo and behold, he had ample samples with him.

It took some persuading to get Melvin out of the van, but the guys drove him home and guided him into bed, but only after he told them his deer story. For Melvin, it had been a very lucky day.

THE NEXT DAY, DONNIE KRUCHTON, my hunting buddy since the 1960s, was walking down the trail with Melvin, when he noticed a culvert beneath the trail. Donnie walked down to look into the culvert and saw something move. He figured it was most likely a

skunk or raccoon. He lay down and shot into the culvert, not re-alizing that Melvin had gone down the other side also to look in the culvert. When Donnie shot, the bullet whistled by Melvin's hand, and he jumped back and said, "Man, was that close!"

COMING UP ONE YEAR AFTER A HEAVY SNOW, we had to park on the trail and walk about 300 feet to our camp. Another few inches fell during the night, and, when we reached the truck, it looked like it had settled down in the snow. Getting closer, we discovered it was missing all four wheel and the battery. Another hunter gave us a ride into town, where we had to buy four used tires plus rims and a new battery.

Joe Holthaus
Pillager, Minnesota

HUNTING HIS WAY

YEARS AGO, AS A YOUNG MAN, my daughter's boyfriend Howard, invited me to hunt deer in South Dakota, near the town of Scenic. Never having hunted mule deer, I was excited.

Arriving a day early, my wife and I rented a motel, and then drove out to scout the deer hunting area. Driving mile after mile, looking for woods, all I saw was acre after acre of prairie grass, a few bushes and an occasional drainage ditch. It looked more like a cow pasture. We didn't see any deer, and wondered where they could hide.

Howard said to meet him at his house at 7:00 a.m. the next morning and got there a few minutes early, Howard was sitting at the table drinking coffee, not even dressed for deer hunting.

I asked, when are we going hunting, that we typically got up at 4:00 a.m. in Minnesota, to get to our stands before day break.

Howard said, "Don't worry. You'll have your deer by nine o'clock." He then began telling big deer stories, and was in no hurry to hunt.

He asked what kind of deer do I wanted? I replied, "A big buck, but when do we leave?"

He replied, "What's your rush? You'll have your buck by nine o'clock! Like I said."

We finally got in his pickup, still in no hurry, and drove out of town, over some field roads, and then across the prairie to a ravine. I began to worry what I had come this far for.

Howard got out his fieldglasses, glassed the ravine and said "It's too foggy. I can't see anything here."

We went back to the truck, he got out the coffee and offered me a cup. A bit frustrated, I said I'd came out here to hunt deer, not drink coffee.

He put his coffee down, and we headed for Hay Draw Canyon. This did look more like a canyon, and I figured it could hold deer. The fog was lifting, and getting out the glasses, Howard spotted three mule bucks, but they were quite a distance down the canyon. He handed me the glasses and said, "Check these out."

I couldn't believe my eyes. "Are these elk?" I had never seen such huge racks.

Shooting a 308 with open sights, it would be too long a shot. I asked Howard "How can we get closer?"

He said, "We'll watch them for a little while, and when they move to bed down, we will head them off."

After a short time they started moving into a deeper part of the canyon. Howard rushed back to the truck, the fastest I had seen him move, and we drove to head them off. Bouncing across the prairie, we came to a fence. Howard yelled, "Get out!"

We crept to the edge of the canyon and settled down, with a good view into the canyon. After a short wait, the mulies came into view, slowing walking towards us. When they got within range, Howard said, "Take the biggest one, the third one."

At the shot, the buck dropped, but quickly got up and rushed after the two fleeing bucks. I kept shooting until I heard a *click*, out of shells, and the buck disappeared.

Howard said, "You hit him good," and pointing to a small bend in the canyon. "Go down there. Get a good view of the canyon and wait. I'll track the deer, and drive it toward you."

After waiting what seemed like an hour, Howard came around the bend and motioned me to come down. As I got near, I could see parts of a massive rack, above the tall grass. The rack was huge, not like Minnesota whitetails. Howard asked, "Should I gut it for you?"

Somewhat insulted, I said, "No, I gut my own deer."

He said, "Now the work comes, getting the buck up to the rim of the canyon."

We were fortunate there were some cow trails along the slope of the canyon, and we had a long rope. I would stand on the cow trails, pull, and he would help pull, as he guided the huge rack through the grass and brush.

With the buck in the back of the truck, I "enjoyed" my first coffee of the day and regained my respect for Howard. I was one happy dude as I returned to Minnesota, with my rack proudly displayed. My friends suggested I have it scored for Boone & Crockett. It had a 28½-inch spread, and I was told it takes a minimum spread of thirty inches for a mule deer.

Harold Voss
St. Cloud, Minnesota

STARTING YOUNG

LIVING ON A FARM NEAR RICE, MINNESOTA, we began hunting at an early age, but back in the 1970s, there weren't the deer we presently have, and it was a challenge to shoot a deer, or even see one.

As our children grew up. Along with their children, we now have twelve or thirteen hunters.

When I was younger, it was important to get a deer, for bragging rights, but now I enjoy assisting the grandkids in their excitement in shooting and seeing the deer and other wildlife. This has taught them to enjoy the outdoors.

At times we have hunted adjacent land, and have learned the travel routes of the deer. We have placed the stands accordingly.

My main enjoyment now is to listen for a shot, and I can usually tell by the sound if the deer was hit, and what stand it was shot from. I then walk over to assist the kids dressing the deer, and showing them the proper method.

I am fortunate my wife, Dorothy, enjoys the outdoors, and quickly took up deer hunting. There were eight guys in our hunting party, and not all of them wanted women hunting with them.

Their first year, Dorothy and two of her friends were put in a ten-by-five-foot stand. It was on the south side of a woods, facing a grass meadow, with a woods about 200 yards to the south. This didn't look like a good hunting spot for them, but they could always do what gals like to do, talk, but quietly.

It was uneventful, with no sounds of shots from the guys, when five deer appeared from the woods across the meadow, running straight at them.

The gals scrambled to get their guns, and pointed them the right direction with one gal standing there saying, "Aren't their tails pretty?"

Nelson Gang.

As the deer got closer, all hell broke out. Despite the barrage of shots, all the deer safely ran off into the distance.

There was a short time of silence, and then loud frustration.

Hearing all the shooting, the guys quickly came over expecting to see some "Brown down" and expecting some embarrassment, as they hadn't scored that morning. Instead of finding the gals standing around a deer, they were huddled beneath the stand.

"Did you get any?" "No." "Did you hit any?" "No." "Where did they come from?" "The woods to the south." "How many were there?" "Five." "FIVE! You had five deer, and didn't even hit one?"

The guys were enjoying the moment, as they tried to ridicule the gals in a polite way, when the gals said, "There comes another one!"

Just like the others, this deer was coming out of the woods, straight at them apparently following the tracks of the original five.

The eight guys all crouched down into the weeds along the woods, like an execution squad as the deer came straight towards them. I told them to wait until they got to about fifty to sixty yards, and then open up. One of the guys put his scope on the deer, at about 150 yards, and wanted to be the "Hero." He fired, and missed. I think he wanted to make a great shot, to show up the gals.

The deer took a ninety degree turn, and raced off, with chunks of dirt flying up all around him as the guys opened fire. It looked like he was running down a plowed furrow. After thirty to forty shots, it ended. Everyone was either out of shells or realizing the distance was too great.

The only noise for the next few seconds was the muffled laughter of the gals behind them.

That night back at camp it was very quiet. There wasn't all the B.S. about their great exploits and shooting skills.

The next day the gals were given much more respect, and

were accepted as members of the group.

Dorothy has since shot many fine deer, including a large bulky buck with an eight-point rack.

At the end of each deer season, we get together for a "Sausage Party." We cut up the meat, grind it, and make our own sausage, with everybody participating.

THERE IS A LONG WETLAND SLOUGH separating some woods on our farm, and two spooked deer attempted to cross it. They leaped and struggled, as they attempted to reach a small patch of grass in the center of the slough. Upon reaching the patch, they stopped briefly and Craig Nelson, in a stand across the slough, dropped one of them.

Retrieving that deer would be difficult, maybe impossible. We could hardly walk out in the water and muck to drag it back. So I went for the duck boat.

Dragging a large adult deer—limp and not dressed—over the side of a small duck boat is no mean trick. After several attempts, and nearly capsizing the boat in the process, I decided to drag it over the front, with the back end of the boat high in the air.

The gang enjoyed my struggle as they cheered and jeered from shore.

I RECEIVED A CALL FROM A LADY WHO was going to demolish an outhouse and asked if I wanted it. It was a poly house, and was small, but I thought it would make a good deer stand.

We removed the stool and cut out windows on all four sides. When we put it on stilts, it made a nice stand. It even had a swinging door, with a spring. We have shot many deer from the stand, thinking the "aroma" may have helped.

Jerome Nelson
Rice, Minnesota

BIG BUCKS ONLY

THERE CAME A TIME IN MY HUNTING when I finally decided that I no longer wanted to shoot the first buck that came along (unless it was big). Most of these were spike bucks and basically walked right up to a hunter. On one occasion a small buck just walked up to me as I was slowly walking our fence line one season. I thought it was a squirrel behind me but it was so loud and close that when I finally turned. He was twenty feet away and staring at me like we were long-lost friends. I crouched down, brought up my gun, and put the cross hairs on his left ear tip. My intentions were to try and keep him alive a few more seasons with a loud education. It was then and there that I set my sights on only shooting larger bucks. I knew that if we were to get some large bucks we need to quit shooting the little ones. I pierced his ear or at least let him know to fear hunters at this time of year. I looked for him for many years to come by checking the ears but never did find one with a pierced ear.

Terry Thorston, Jacob Hageman, and Brad Hageman.

It was at this time that the hunting group implemented a "shoot only if the rack is outside the ears" rule. I do all the food plots, cabin preparation, trail clearing, and stand maintenance, so it was easy to make the rule. The one exception was in regarding our younger hunters and my older brother. The new hunters were allowed to shoot what they wanted as a way to get hooked on the sport. Fifteen years of food plots and passing on the little ones was paying off. If only I could get the neighbors and the brother to follow suit, we could come across some trophy bucks.

Two years ago my friend Terry shot a monster of a buck from the base of the cold stand. He was headed out to the stand and we were going to make a drive, but he never made it into the stand. He was thirty feet away and heard the buck snort and saw him run. The shot was a tricky one, but he downed him. He then climbed the stand to get a better view of the swamp where the buck fell. Shortly after I showed up, he pointed out into the swamp. I found a trail and started walking out. From over seventy yards away, I could see the rack, and it was very impressive even from that distance. The twenty-inch spread was easily seen sticking

up through the grass of the berry bog. The scoring was done months later and was at 157. The buck's body was small in proportion to the rack. This makes two years in a row that Terry has gotten the Big One.

Brad Hageman
Foley, Minnesota

Terry Thorston and Brad Hageman.

MEMORIES

This past year, 2009, in our deer stand for three weekends we did see a nice button buck on opening day running by the south side, headed west. He stopped for a short while, looked right at us, and was off in a flash. That was it for the year, but as I said, just seeing a deer is a success.

That button buck stopped right in our shooting lane to the west. It reminded me of that eight-point buck I shot at and wounded the year before and never recovered. Reflecting on that experience, I was using my 30-30 lever-action rifle. I was thinking after that shooting experience, maybe just maybe if I had my 300 Winchester magnum bolt-action rifle with me and was using that big rifle, I could have downed that eight-point buck, but I no longer had that rifle. I bought that big rifle for hunting moose and elk. The last hunting trip I took with that 300 Win mag was on a guided deer hunt in Manitoba a few years back with my son-in-law, Todd. Great trip, saw many deer but only one monster at about 500 yards. I fired three rounds at that nice deer, but I didn't score. I thought my shoulder was going to drop on the ground. "That's it," I said to Todd. After injuring my rotator cuff falling on ice a few years ago, I couldn't handle the kick of that 300 Win mag anymore. It was time to sell that rifle and use my 30-30 for deer hunting—less kick.

I was talking to my youngest son, Brian, after that experience with the kick of the 300 Win mag and told him that I was going to sell that rifle. Brian was talking to my oldest son, Gary, about my decision to sell the 300 win mag. My son Gary called me up and said, "Dad, I hear you're going to sell the 300 Win mag. Well you can't do that. That rifle has too many memories."

I told Gary, "Well I own the 300 Win mag, and I can sell it if I want to." Gary then said to me, "Dad, I have a question for you. How do you feel about pre-paying my inheritance?"

"Oh, I get it, you want that rifle! Let me think about that for a while." After giving that idea some thought, I said to myself, *Sure, that's where it belongs. Pass it on to the next generation.* For Christmas that year I wrapped the shells from the 300 Win mag and put them under the tree. I had cleaned the rifle up and had it in the case in the closet, ready for Christmas Day. When Gary opened up the package of shells, he looked on the butt end to see what it said. In plain language it read, "300 Win Mag." Gary knew what was coming up, and he wasn't lost for words very often, but this time, he was all choked up. We caught all of this action on film. What a great feeling passing this 300 Win mag to the next generation. Gary said, "Dad, I'll take really good care of this rifle and Brian can use it too."

Our deer stand has nice swivel chairs along with a small table that we use for putting our lunch on. It's a good place to put the cribbage board and cards. They help pass the time. We have binoculars hanging on the wall and ear muffs for when shooting. They sure cut the rifle noise down.

One day while sitting in our deer stand, Big Pete said to me, "Look outside. There's a bear. Oh, no, not a bear. It's a dog, a Doberman running through the woods." I don't know where that dog came from, but it sure surprised us.

Vince Shallbetter
Mora, Minnesota

OVERCOMING

I was born on June 22, 1966, with a very rare syndrome known as Aperts. Aperts left me with severe physical disabilities to my hands, feet bones, and head. I have three and one-half fingers and a thumb on each hand with one and one-half fingers fused together. My fingers only bend slightly where they come out from my hand. Now I do have five toes, but they are all fused together on each foot. The syndrome also affected my head so that I look strange to most people. But thanks to a new procedure that a doctor at the university knew about, along with another specialist at the University Hospital of Minnesota, he was able to fix that. It was two separate operations, but they where able to make my face more normal. I have had over twenty operations in my life mostly for my syndrome. One of the first ones I had was to have some of my fingers separated because my fingers other than my thumb were fused together at birth. Then my last two were in 2004 and 2007 when I had to have both shoulders replaced. Because I was given square shoulder balls when I was born, so after forty years I had just bone on bone. But in spite of being born with a few challenges, I haven't let them stop me from leading a normal life thanks to my great parents. When I was growing up I could never say that I couldn't do something with out trying it first. Then if I

couldn't do something in a normal way, I needed to find my own way of doing whatever I needed to do. Thanks to my parents and my speech therapist, who had to fight for me to get me into a normal classroom with I started school, I graduated from high school in 1986. After high school, I went on to college and graduated in 1989 with a B.S. in Mass Communications. Then in 1996, I went back to technical college and graduated from their year-long course in Water and Waste Water Technology.

I owe a lot to my parents and was also very lucky to be born a very stubborn and determined individual. When someone tells me I can't do something or that I shouldn't do something because I have handicaps, that makes me even more determined to do whatever it is. I am also very lucky to have parents who loved the outdoors. They taught me to hunt and fish. Just to say that I have a few trophies on the wall isn't saying much. I don't have a lot of big racks of the bucks I've shot, but to me everything that I shoot is a trophy. The thing that makes me happy is that I am able to feed my family.

I am also very thankful to my parents that they let me go after my dreams. Shortly after I had my head reconstruction operation, one of my best friends got me into Bicycle Motocross racing. I raced BMX for four years but was never good at it because I didn't have the quick speed needed in it. But that was all right because I was having fun trying to do it. When I was nineteen, I got into road cycling and I am still doing that today. I have won many races over the years. I am entering my twenty-fifty year of racing in 2010. But now I just do time trials in cycling because I broke my right hip in a criterium bike race in 2004. Now I'm getting into doing triathalons and running races.

About four to five years ago I took my first hunt with a cross bow, because I just had the right shoulder replaced the year before and couldn't pull back my compound bow anymore. Archery season started out okay in that I was seeing deer almost every night, but nothing was coming close enough to give me a shot. I talked with the landowner to see if it was all right if I could move my portable ladder stand there. Because the deer were coming out to the field in this other spot about 100 yards from where I was. He said I could, so my dad and I moved my stand. A few nights later a nice doe came within my range, at least that's what I thought. But, after watching the deer for twenty minutes, I was a little shaky and missed the doe. The next morning when I came off the stand, I had a note on my car from the landowner, telling me that he found another spot for me on another field.

I'm right handed but shoot left handed, making it hard for me to move to my left to shoot. The owner said that I could build a stand, so my dad and I went the next day to built one. That night, I sat on the new stand and hadn't seen a thing and it was getting dark. But then I heard the brush crack and saw movement. The next moment out stepped a nice deer, and he stopped at my twenty-yard marker that I had stuck in the ground. It was just a stick that I had used to mark the distance off, but it told me what I needed to know. I quickly took a second to think because my dad told me to wait for the deer to get out into the field more. I then told myself that I should take the shot now because I knew that I was nailing the bull's eye in practice at twenty yards. I quickly pulled up and saw that the deer did have antlers but I hadn't counted the points. So I aimed and pulled the trigger. The deer just stood there a moment, then walked off. Once he got to the woods, he started running. So I called my parents, and they came, but by then it was already dark. We left and came back in the morning. We found the arrow, and it had good sign on it that I had hit the deer, in fact, it had gone all the way through the deer. But there was very little sign to track. Thanks to my mother, we tracked the deer and eventually walked up to it. I was able to claim a nice eight-point buck.

I also used to rifle hunt, and the last deer I shot with my rifle was an eight-pointer. My parents had the head mounted for me. I think that I shot that in 2003. In 2004 I had the broken hip and the right shoulder replaced. I was really happy when I got the nine-pointer because again I knew that it was a buck when I shot. But like the first eight-pointer that I got with my cross bow. I didn't take time to count the tines or to see how big the rack was. Because all I was trying to do was to feed me and my parents. But I don't rifle hunt anymore because now my dad and I head to Texas in October and are winter Texans for six months. But I might rifle hunt some day again. I'll see if my left shoulder can handle it. But I'm not worrying about it as long as I can hunt with my cross bow.

Now I know that I have my physical disabilities, but I don't see myself as handicapped. I just see myself as a normal person who has had to overcome a few things in his life. I also know that I will accomplish many more goals than I have set for myself, because I know that anything is possible if a person has a dream to do it.

Shayne Stiller
Waskish, Minnesota

THIRTY-EIGHT STANDS

W E HAVE THREE DIFFERENT PROPERTIES that have a variety of well-placed ground blinds, portable stands, and tree stands. Two of these are separated by a mile of state land and the third is four miles away. The property that is furthest away has a high oak ridge and swampy floating bogs surrounding it. One winter we made a tri-pod stand out in a spruce-floating bog because none of the trees would support a stand. It was my most challenging one as I had to snowmobile in all the timbers and wood from a mile away. It was assembled in the winter time and I had to make sure that it would not sink into the mossy bog material come spring time also. The location is such that it is impossible to get to without trekking through some very difficult terrain. This stand is called the Bog Stand and has claimed a few wet legs as the unfortunate break through are inevitable.

Every stand we have has a name. Some are named after my children if they helped to make it. Other names reflect the materials built with and or locations. Some of these include the Cold Stand, Kill Me Stand, Oak Stand

The Dream Stand

Rebar Stand with Alainas up in it and Jacob down below.

or Meg's Stand, Ironing Board Stand, Silo Stand, Comfy Chair Stand, Birch Tree Stand, and many that are just directional. NE, SW, or North Fence Stand. Each spot is picked upon years of sightings, and aerial photos are used to choose avenues that will have good deer movement. I have loved every one of them as each means many hours afield with my kids. Having so many spots to choose from is difficult sometimes as there are only five to seven who hunt regularly. I will choose the Cold Stand when it is snowing, not because there will be deer, but because it is so beautiful to look out over the 14,000 acres of open swamps and fields to the north.

For many years now one of my six kids will be along so I have to choose stands that will handle two people, or are within sight of each other as they are young hunters. I recently have taken up muzzle loading as a way to get some "me" time as the regular season has been all about my children and their successful hunts.

There are many days we are not sure where to go as there are so many stands to choose from. My brother always goes to the same spot, whereas I tend to pick sites I feel will be productive. If one area has not produced a big one in a couple years, then I will hunt there. One year a dream lead me to hunt an area. On one such occasion I dreamt the location I should hunt and was really in a conundrum as to whether I should or not. It was not my typical spot. It was close to the Soo Line Trail and human activity. I did hunt it but not from the vantage point in the dream. Instead, I went into the woods 200 feet and could not see the field as in my dream. When I got out there that morning, I just felt it would be better to go into the woods on the trail. After two hours of

Silo Stand

Jon's Corner Stand

watching this spot, I moved to the field of dreams. I sat there for five minutes and out came a herd of deer. There were no big bucks as in my dream, but maybe I should have been there the whole morning.

We have now put a stand in that location also. It was put up hastily last season and needs to be done differently to make it safer. As the years go by, I wonder if there are too many stands and the bigger bucks are staying away. But then this past season was the hardest hunt for me ever. I was overdue for hip replacements and could not get into many of my stands. We made an easier stand for me to get into using a stairway from another stand I had previously made for my father-in-law. This stand is called the Dam Stand as there is an old beaver dam below me. With that taken care of, I decided that I had to give my favorite stand to my oldest son. So, I gave my bog stand to my son and wanted to make sure he knew how to get to it so

Mall's Pine Stand

he would not drown. The trail to this stand is full of obstacles that are hard to navigate when there is daylight, let alone in the pre-dawn hours. I have marked my trail by cutting branches and chipping the bark away from the sides of trees that lead to and back, for early morning and late night travel. It is always wet and there is always a beaver trench that has to be navigated delicately. If you

Jon and Ben by the hunting shack.

stay to close to the pond, you run the risk of falling through the floating bog as the ground is thin. If you go too far away from the pond, the deer bedded on the ridge will scent or see you. As I was showing my twenty-year-old son the trail, he was saying, "I know the way, dad." As we walked further I told him. "Here is where you move away from the pond and into the tamaracks." He said, "I go this way a little farther before going in." The ensuing argument was about safety and how treacherous it was ahead. I finally said, "Go for it." His very next step had me laughing harder than ever before and had him making a very sheepish face as one leg sank three feet into the muck of the bog. He got up and had a nervous laugh until his next step landed him in another split with his other leg getting soaked. After a brief moment of self-composure, he said, "I'll follow you." Youth They have to learn on their own, I guess. The bog stand is usually my opening morning stand and did not get hunted much this past year, so I will go for it this coming season. But, then again, I may have another dream that states otherwise.

Brad Hageman
Foley, Minnesota

Alaina.

HIGH FLYER

Otter Tail Power Company received a call from a customer saying, "My power is out. When you come to fix it, be sure to bring a truck with a tall enough bucket to remove the deer." The customer service representative, prudently trying to gather information to help diagnose the problem asked, "What deer?" The customer replied, "There is a deer on top of one of the electric poles on Highway 2 about half a mile west of Leeds, North Dakota.

The service representative tried desperately to pull herself together and not laugh in front of the customer. She replied, "We'll dispatch someone right away to investigate the power outage. Thank you for your call."

The customer service representative proceeded to share the funny story with her coworkers in the office and they all had a good laugh. Well, lo and behold, the serviceman who repaired the outage problem stopped by the customer service office the following day with pictures. Sure enough, a deer had been hit by a train and landed on top of a distribution feeder pole!

Dick Nordquist
St. Cloud

"Hot" Stand

I HAVE HUNTED DEER FOR FORTY-THREE YEARS and hunt with a wonderful bunch of guys who invited me to hunt the Big Woods. We camped out for ten days in northeast Minnesota in the Big Woods, and even bigger swamps. I bought a six-foot pod stand, added a camo wrap around it, a can holder, carpet on floor, and a Black Cat upright catalytic heater. I split a black rubber tarp strap down the middle, stretched it over the base, secured the ends to the pod stand and keep warm all day long. This heater came with a black plastic cover, so it didn't get wet when not in use.

On opening day, my stand was at the edge of a wooded finger point that led to a swampy area. I saw no action for five hours and decided to go back to camp and have a bowl of soup. Typically I hate leaving my stand at all, but I was hungry. I shut down the heater and, like always, kept my hand above it to tell when it cooled down, then put the cap on. While sitting in camp, I just couldn't take not being on the stand so I only ate half a bowl of soup and went back.

When I arrived at my stand my jaw dropped. There was a fifty-foot-diameter burned area in the swamp, and my stand was still smoking. Had I turned the heater up, and not off? I put the cap on the heater, lifted the shooting rail with the camo around it, climbed down the stand and left for camp. The black plastic cap melted and started on fire, igniting the camo, which burned the seat cushion and back rest, which dropped onto the carpet and burned it. Then the fire fell through the pod stand onto an orange backpack I carried out which contained three more one-pound propane bottles, and some other hunting equipment. The fire fell on the backpack, and it went into flames, which released the pressure valve on the propane tanks, scorching one leg of the stand and starting a smoldering grass fire. I put out the remaining smoking bog and just stared. The propane tanks had not exploded but they were bulging before the relief valve opened.

Dragging my sorry tail back to camp, I was met by some other party members who asked why I was back at camp so soon. How do you tell your friends and fellow hunters you just burned up your stand and nearly caused a forest fire?

Mark Hennagir
New York Mills, Minnesota

HUNTING GREEN

MY DEER STANDS ARE MADE FROM OLD COMBINES. I have made four of them. They are all metal except the floor, which is made from two-by-sixes and can be replaced by simply lifting them out. I attach old carpet to the sides so if I touch them with your rifle it doesn't make noise. They are just under thirteen feet high, so I can travel on roads and get under the electric wires. They are made so I can stand on the pole and put my rifle on the floor so I don't have to climb up with my weapon, and they are wide enough to take a kid or two along in order to teach them about hunting. My stand is in a wooded area where four old logging trails meet. I can see about fifty yards in four directions.

One of the best features of my deer stand is the truck mirrors. With these I can see behind me without moving so I don't startle the deer. My very first year in my deer stand with mirrors,

I saw a doe enter the trail in front of me. She was looking in my direction. I looked up in the mirror and saw the buck behind me, but they both decided to continue on into the woods. About half an hour later, the doe appeared back in the same location. I looked in the mirror, and

the buck was there also. But this time he came to meet his doe and came right by my stand. It was an easy shot. I'm glad I had the mirrors to see that he was there. In 2008 I got an eight-point and a ten-point buck from the same stand.

James Mattfeld
Frazee, Minnesota

Mark, Erin, and Jim.

Turkeys, Pingo, Then Deer

I HAD BEEN PREPARING FOR THIS DEER archery season for the latter half of the year, but I'd been dreaming of it for many of my past twenty-seven years, sitting with my dad in the woods since age fourteen.

The chance for this dream began four years ago, as a result of turkeys on our farm near Belgrade. A turkey hunter, Corwin Hoffbeck, came to our farm asking permission to hunt turkeys on our land. Dad gave him permission. He hunted our land for four years, always being considerate of the opportunity.

This last spring, 2009, I was sitting outside with my dog Pingo, when Corwin (C.J.) stopped by to pick up his turkey decoys. As C.J. drove out of the yard, he was playfully being chased by Pingo.

Pingo had a history of epileptic seizures, and, as he raced along the car, he had a seizure and fell against the wheel, then was

Corwin, Nate, and Pingo.

thrown to the ground. C.J. heard the thump and saw Pingo fall and lie on the ground. C.J. stopped and ran back to Pingo. The dog was slowly regaining consciousness. C.J. picked him up and carried him back to me, apologizing. Pingo had only minor injuries.

C.J. later came back to check on Pingo, bringing him treats. As we were talking, C.J. asked if I would like to go archery hunting for deer. I said I would love to hunt, but I had no use of my arms or legs.

I am disabled, a condition called Duchene Muscular Dystrophy. It affects my muscles and leaves me limited movement. I can feel in my arms and legs, so I am able to stand the cold. I've had it all my life, and at age eight I went into a wheelchair. Since the age of fourteen, I have always enjoyed sitting in the woods with my dad, enjoying watching deer and other creatures of nature, never expecting I would one day be able to hunt them.

Scope.

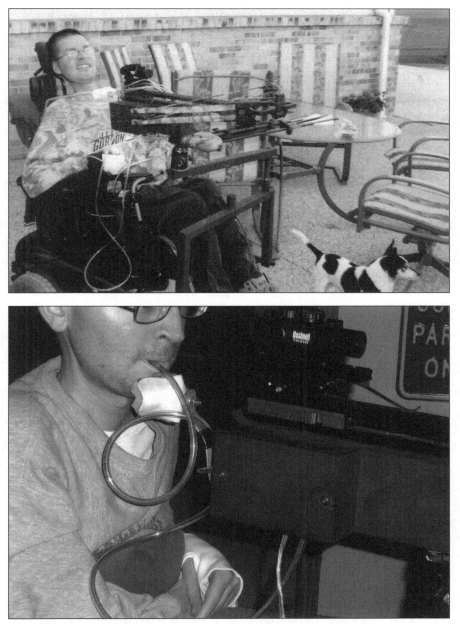

Top: Complete equipment. Bottom: The control tube to release the arrow.

About a month later, my mother, Linda, got a call from C.J. He was at Cabelas, to meet with a quadriplegic about equipment he had used to bow hunt deer.

As the months went by, C.J. took measurements of my wheelchair and began assembling the necessary equipment to mount my bow to it. The framework to support my bow started with two short pieces of pipe welded to a piece of square tubing. This was welded to a clamp to attach to the frame of my wheelchair. Two pieces of tubing about thirty inches long were cut. They were to slide through the two short pieces. The longer pieces were then welded to a piece of square tubing. This formed the support to hold my bow, much like the frame on a tractor loader. The longer pipe then had a piece of square tubing welded to it to form an L-shaped bracket used to adjust the bow. A camera mount was bolted to the L bracket with a "quick release" that also connected my bow to the mount, like a camera tripod.

On my bow, I have a regular Red-Dot scope. A bolt on the mount allowed me to raise my bow bracket to the proper height or angle and tighten the bolt.

To load my bow, someone helps me by placing his foot on the bar in the front, holding it forcefully to the ground while he draw it back. He then slowly pulls the bowstring back until he hears the trigger lock it in place. He slides the bolt in the track with the fin down, all the way back to the trigger. Then he puts it on safe. It is then attached to my wheelchair.

The control tube I use is medical-grade plastic tubing. When I suck on the tube, this activates the solenoid, which is connected to a car battery. The solenoid then pulls the trigger on the bow. This can only happen after the safety switch on the bow and on the solenoid have been turned on. The person who assists me has to do this.

When I'm prepared, I have vertical sight adjustment but I'm limited to about thirty degrees of horizontal adjustment.

When a deer comes into view, I lean forward to place the air tube in my mouth, placing my chin in a chin mount behind the scope. I can aim my bow by moving my chin.

Getting prepared to shoot is tedious, and I will only shoot at a standing deer to avoid a crippling shot at a moving target.

When all is ready, I turn on the two safeties, one on the bow, and one on the solenoid. They both have to be on before the bow can be fired. The person who sits with me has to switch on the safeties. I suck in on the tube and the arrow is on the way.

C.J. prepared me well, with hours of practice and setting out five trail cams. He would check the cameras and place the pictures on my computer. We had pictures of does and fawns and at least three decent bucks.

C.J. was an avid hunter, but he spent his time taking me hunting two or three times a week during the archery season. During that time, I saw many deer, some close enough to shoot, but I never fired a shot. I wanted to wait for a good shot, not take a "chance shot" that could cripple a deer.

At times it was frustrating as it would take perfect timing, and several times as I was nearly set, the deer would move on. I was still grateful for this opportunity to hunt.

The weekly hunts were enjoyable, but I yearned for success. The colder weather made hunting more difficult, but I was determined to succeed.

What would probably be my last hunt of the year, my

Left to right: Jim Nelson, Corwin Hoffbeck "C.I.," Nate Nelson, Pete Mohs, and John Nelson.

dad took me out on the Sunday before Christmas. It was pretty cold that afternoon, with eight to ten inches of snow on the ground. We got set up to hunt about 3:30.

What makes it difficult to shoot is that I had a greater vertical angle of sight, but could move my chin and scope only in a thirty-degree arc. This greatly reduced my shooting angle.

As my hunting season was about to end, two fawns walked out, saw my decoy, stopped, snorted, and ran back into the woods. The decoy served two purposes, to possibly attract deer and to "unload" my bow at the end of the day.

After a few seconds, the doe stepped out, at about thirty yards, apparently checking out what had upset her fawns. The decoy got her attention, as she stood and observed, giving me the time I required.

Careful not to draw her attention, my dad, Jim, helped sight in the bow, as the moment I had waited so long for was here. I took a deep breath, sucked in, and the arrow released. There was a *plat*. Success!

At first I was in shock. I couldn't believe it had happened. It took several minutes before I understood what had happened and got excited. I was sure my dad could hear my heart beating.

After calling my mother, the first call was to C.J., the person who had made all of this possible. I will forever be grateful to him. I also want to thank my parents, sister, Keshia, brother, Dustin, and his wife, Angela, and their sons, Wyatt and Lane. They have always inspired and assisted me. Also thanks to turkeys and Pingo.

Nate Nelson
Belgrade, Minnesota

CASA DEL DEER SLAYER

MY NAME IS KELLI AMELL AND I AM a thirty-five-year-old wife and mother of two little girls, ages four and five. I began deer hunting at the age of twenty-three. My (then new) husband, Scott, loved deer hunting, so I wanted to experience the sport he was so passionate about. I thought it would be great if we could share that passion as we grew old together. The first two years, I hunted at my grandmother's farm with my father in Mankato, Minnesota. My husband and I own 160 acres in Nimrod, Minnesota, that had been passed down in his family, but it was a "guys only" affair. I used Scott's old 20-gauge youth model Remington he'd hunted with when he was twelve. It had no iron sights, just a bead at the end of the barrel. After hunting in Mankato for two years, my grandmother sold her farm, and I was reluctantly allowed to hunt on our land in Nimrod.

My first stand was a small box that sat on the ground in a small clearing about a quarter mile into the woods. I had pretty good luck the next six years, always able to get a deer. My seventh year hunting, I was able to shoot a beautiful ten-point buck. I'll never forget the looks on everyone's faces when they saw that deer. They said it was the biggest deer

taken off of the property in the thirty years the land had been in the family—it still holds the record today. The "girl" comments stopped, and I finally felt as if I belonged to the hunting party and wasn't someone who had to be tolerated because I was Scott's wife. Respect was finally earned.

The year after I shot the ten-point buck, Scott decided it was time for us to build a new stand for me—he said I deserved it with the title. He let me design it from the ground up. We built it in our garage together and hauled it up north. The entire hunting party turned out to help get it out into the woods. My stand is six feet by six feet with twelve-foot roofing trusses. The eight panels (two on each side) folded up to keep out wind and rain—if the weather is bad, I can put one or two up to block out the elements. AND I have a toilet seat (and toilet paper holder). I paint murals part time on the side, mostly children's rooms and borders. I decided to paint my own version of "camouflage." There are 500 hand-painted leaves and another 500 hand-painted wooden leaves glued on to give it more dimension. The cedar shingles are color coordinated with the rest of the "camo palette."

Two years later I shot another huge eight-point buck, the second largest deer harvested off our land. Both the ten-pointer and the eight-pointer are hanging on the wall. Now my nickname is Annie Oakley, and I sport a pink "girls shoot better" decal on my Suburban. I have a passion all my own for this amazing sport. Neither my husband nor I can sleep the week prior to opener.

Scott and I have been together fifteen years now, and one of the best decisions I ever made was to try to share in his passion to hunt. I am so grateful to him to be willing to share the experience with me . . . I don't think many guys would have. Now it is something we enjoy together, and I hope some day our daughters will join us.

Kelli Amell
Oak Grove, Minnesota

WHO SMELLS?

WE GOT UP AT 4:30 A.M. TO ENJOY Henry's breakfast (greasy eggs and bacon). After George and I finished dressing for the morning hunt, he decided he needed to use the outdoor bathroom.

He pulled his one-piece orange snowmobile suit with hood down and squatted to do his job. As he finished and came closer to the camper, a sharp smell came with him, and I asked if he'd crapped in his pants or didn't wipe. He barked, "No!" I asked if he'd stepped in it on his way back. Again he barked a negative.

George and I started into the woods on the logging trail, but that smell wasn't going away, and I was tempted to ask again if he'd had some trouble with the snowmobile suit while he was relieving himself.

As we split up, George stayed on the edge and I proceeded into the woods. About 8:30, I walked to the road and back to the camper where Henry and Doug were sleeping. I then walked to

George, where we had split up earlier and discussed checking out the woods on the other side of the road across from the camper. After walking towards the clearing, George wanted to climb a tree and look around. I took his gun while he climbed into the tree and thought I could take that opportunity to relieve myself. George hollered down from his perch in the tree that he could smell me up there. I finished and went over to help George down out of the tree. That's when I noticed something in his hood. Closer inspection revealed that it was his morning deposit. Laughing hard, I unzipped his hood and showed it to him. He stared a moment, then said he had been standing earlier and was getting chilled. He had considered pulling on the hood, but hadn't because he thought his movements might spook a deer.

George and Julie Ruter
Willmar, Minnesota

RESERVED PARKING

OUR OPEN-AIR OUTHOUSE NEAR Nashwauk, Minnesota, serves as a deer stand for shot spells throughout the deer season. It overlooks a stand of pine, and the camp rule is, "Never go to the shitter without a loaded rifle because someday someone's gonna bag a buck!"

We haven't bagged one yet, but we've heard deer moving through the pines. When one moves closer while nature is calling, we'll mount the rack on a toilet seat.

Ron Flett
Maple Grove

QUIET GUN

ROWING UP LOVING NATURE and spending countless hours in the outdoors, hunting and fishing, little did I realize the effect of being diagnosed with multiple sclerosis at the age of sixteen would have on my life.

It was gradual, but many years ago, now at the age of fifty, I am confined to a wheelchair. Growing up and being self-dependent, I found it difficult to ask for any assistance.

I was only able to continue my enjoyment of deer hunting and other outdoor activities through the loving support of my family, friends, and civic group dedicated to assisting persons who are physically challenged.

One of my most memorable deer hunt was in 2006, which was made possible through the efforts of the D.N.R., "Capable Partners," and the "Wheeling Sportsmen" Organization. They provided full equipment and support for a two-day deer hunt for twelve physically challenged hunters.

The hunt was held on 240 acres of private property owned by Tom Lenneman, a longtime supporter of outdoor activities. The land was located on the south side of St. Cloud, along the Mississippi River, within the city limits.

Well before sunup, we went by A.T.V. to our hunting location. Each hunter was provided with a mentor who would help with the setup, and stay with the hunter. My mentor was my younger brother, Troy, who I had mentored as he was growing up.

Troy set up a doe decoy out about forty yards, and then assisted me in my wheelchair to get set for the hunt. We overlooked a beautiful wooded area, with the beautiful Mississippi River visible in the distance.

I was hunting in a canvas ground blind, with a cumbersome shotgun, having a five- to six-foot barrel, a usual barrel being twenty-six to twenty-eight inches.

The quiet gun.

Inside city limits, we used a "quiet gun," with a barrel five to six feet long and shoots a special shell. The gun is equipped with a scope and a stabilizer bar and the barrel extends outside the blind. The gun has a quieter report, causing less concern among neighbors.

Sitting in a wheelchair, my only vertical alignment comes from raising or lowering my head, and horizontal alignment by sliding the gun barrel on the stabilizer bar. I enjoyed the challenge.

After "set up," we sat quietly, waiting for light and legal shooting hours. It was only a short time before a doe appeared, thirty yards away, seemingly out of nowhere. She stopped, eyed the decoy, and slowly moved towards it. She approached it, seemed to nuzzle it and then slowly moved away.

I had only a few seconds, not enough time to sight in. As the doe moved away, Troy used the "doe bleat." The doe would momentarily stop, but still didn't give me enough time to sight in. At about sixty yards, she turned broadside, stopped, and gave me the time I needed. At the shot, the deer dropped.

There were several seconds of silence as Troy and I were in disbelief that it finally had happened. I believe Troy was as excited as I was, as I had mentored him when he was in his youth, he now had the opportunity to return the favor. I was allowed to shoot two deer, and the second day a group of four deer walked by our stand. I believe I could have gotten a shot off, but none were bucks.

There were signs of large bucks in the area, and I was hoping to beat my present record of twelve points.

I was the only hunter of the twelve to shoot a deer, but they all saw deer, and there was several missed shots. Despite their lack of success, they were all excited and told stories of "What if . . ."

We were all thankful. For many of us, this was a once in a lifetime hunt. We were grateful to the sponsors and mentors for their time and effort spent to make this hunt possible.

Dan Vetsch
St. Cloud, Minnesota

IN THE CORN

FTER HUNTING DEER SINCE 1948, 2008 was my first year of hunting over a cornfield, and I experienced some difficulties.

I was hunting from and eight-foot box stand, about thirty feet from a field of picked corn. Even though it was picked, with many stalks and leaves still upright, I still thought I could see easily into the field. Wrong!

I didn't realize how short deer were, only thirty-two to forty inches at the shoulder. That's less than three feet to three and one-half feet, and with their heads down feeding, that's it. Despite being only sixty yards away, I didn't see the six-point buck until he raised his head. That was his mistake.

The next year, I hunted the same field, my brother-in-law's farm north of St. Cloud, with unpicked corn, from a twelve-foot stand. To get some site/shooting lanes, I got permission to bend over or break off some corn stalks (above the ears, of course, so as not to affect the harvest). I left the first six rows on the outside edge of the field to make the deer feel more secure.

I placed four sight lines in a wagon spoke pattern. If a deer crossed a lane, I hoped I could stop it with a grunt or get it at the next lane. The lanes were four to five feet wide, and I bent over the stalks in the direction of the rows. My center sight line was about eighty yards, straight out from my stand, crossing over the rows. This was my longest line, as it went slightly up hill, giving me my longest view.

Between my stand and the standing corn was a twenty-foot width of grass and weeds, which was often the deer's travel route. To my right was a twenty-four-inch oak, which was my stand support, but it also blocked my view from deer coming in from my right.

At 8:30 a.m. a doe ran into the sight line from the right and stopped abruptly, looking nervous and excited. It looked back

the way it had come, then down my sight line. Then it quickly bounded toward me, leaping over the bent-over corn stalks. After about thirty yards, it made an abrupt right turn in to a corn row.

By the sound and movements of the corn stalks, it appeared to stop after about twenty feet. Up twelve feet and looking into a slight rise, at forty yards, I couldn't see the deer. I could see a slight shadow area, but not a profile. Knowing it wouldn't stand long, I took a shot at what I assumed would be the chest area.

At the shot, I saw a slight movement from three or four corn stalks, and then quiet. After about ten seconds, I saw a slight movement from another corn stalk, but no indication of a deer moving down the row.

After the shot, I expected one of three things: The doe would run down the corn row, stand still to figure out where the shot came from, or, if hit, drop, struggle and knock down some corn stalks. I envisioned this last option to be a lot more activity than I saw.

I looked at my watch and decided to wait one hour before investigating, watching the area, waiting for movement. Intent on the spot where the doe had been, I wasn't glancing around the tree to check for other deer coming from my right.

About ten minutes later, a fawn came in from my right and raced down the weed area to my left. It would have been a difficult shot as the animal was bounding both vertically and side to side. Chances were I would more likely cripple it than kill it, if I hit it at all. I decided not to shoot.

As I watched the fawn disappear into the corn, a nine-point buck raced by my stand in full pursuit. I got off a shot at about sixty yards, hitting the buck in the spine. It dropped, doing a complete somersault in the process. Looking back, I still saw no movement from the doe.

After waiting ten minutes, I went to dress out the buck. With all the commotion of the second shot and climbing down

The spot just off the corner of the doe's eye is where I hit her.

from my stand, I knew the doe was either dead or just plain gone.

I waited several minutes, fighting suspense. I was enjoying the excitement, not wanting to rush what probably was disappointment. Approaching the area where I thought the deer should be lying, I found nothing. Five more rows, and again, nothing. Another four rows, elation.

The doe lay in a fetal position, between the rows, having disturbed none of the standing corn. It had dropped at the shot, with no struggle. My question—that of all hunters—where had I hit it? I knew it had been running to my left, so I expected to see a wound on the left side. It was lying on its right side, and I sure saw no wound there. I turned the deer over and looked it over head to tail. No wound. Rolling it over again, I saw no exit wound . . . no wound at all. Still it was down.

I gutted the deer and found no sign of internal injury. I raised the deer to drain the cavity and noticed a small spot of red hair about an inch below the right eye. (See arrow on photo opposite.) I took a closer look, poked the spot with my finger and discovered it was a bullet hole. Shooting a 30-06, and never having shot a deer in the head, I would have expected the head to be shattered, but it looked pretty much untouched except for the bloody hair.

But the wound was on the right side of the head. The only thing I could figure out was that the doe had to be looking back over her shoulder at the time of the shot, maybe at the buck following the fawn.

This was November 7, 2009. The last deer season I missed was fifty years earlier, November 7, 1959, my wedding day. In 1959, the cost of a deer license was $3.00, and a "dear" license was $5.00.

I made the right choice. Yep, I had my bonus tag.

Bob Erickson
St. Cloud, Minnesota

About the Author

Bob Erickson grew up in Central Minnesota. In his youth, he spent time hunting, fishing, and trapping. He's continued his interest in the outdoors and hunting to this day. This is the first in a series of books that celebrates the stories and experiences of fellow sports-people. He lives in St. Cloud, Minnesota, with his wife.